The Working Woman

A Male Manager's View

Ray A. Killian

AMA

AMERICAN MANAGEMENT ASSOCIATION

To the two women in my life—
My wife, Betty, and my daughter, Ann

International standard book number: 0-8144-5248-5
Library of Congress catalog card number: 76-138567

FIRST PRINTING

The
Working
Woman

Preface

THIS book provides specific, practical guides to male and female leaders for achieving maximum harmony and performance results with women. Its premise rests heavily on the fact that there are pertinent, job-related differences between men and women; that these can be identified; and that with appropriate leadership these differences can benefit all concerned. It demonstrates that women can be understood and their behavior on the job can be predicted; that women have tremendous potential for both job contribution and leadership; and that programs can be developed for maximizing their achievements.

The text provides an understanding of fundamental principles for motivating women to perform effectively on the job. It seeks to minimize the anxiety and uncertainties sometimes associated with female job behavior and to provide dependable guides for amiable relationships and the attainment of desired results.

It recognizes the rapidly growing number and influence of women as employees, supervisors, customers, stockholders, and molders of the total business and cultural environment. The significance of this is clear: Both males and females who are concerned with managing a company, manufacturing a product, selling a service, and being employed as well as employing and supervising other people must master the special skills associated with female interests, potential, and motivational responses. To ignore uniquely female qualities is to court management failure and economic suicide. Coping with these qualities may be frustrating, but the effort can prove to be both interesting and rewarding.

Personal work experience with women, survey results, and special research interviews have demonstrated that women have both the dedication and the serious desire for achievement in the business world. They are earnest seekers of knowledge and are willing to expend the effort necessary to advance in business as people, not as women per se. At the conclusion of a tape-recorded group discussion with leading female executives from a variety of organizations, the consensus was, "Now, let's hear what the men have to say. We know that they have more influence on the operation of business than we do, so we want to hear their opinions. We need to know what they think we can do to contribute more and get ahead faster." A transcript of this group interview is in Appendix B.

The writing of this book has been approached with justifiable trepidation. I realize that many areas covered, facts stated, guidelines recommended, and statements made regarding women are subject to differences of opinion, which can sometimes be emotional. In fact, some experts might not agree with the premise of this book, which is that a special book about women is necessary and desirable. However, my own survey of hundreds of male and female executives revealed that 98 percent agree that such a book is desirable.

There will be exceptions to the conclusions stated. Where people are concerned, very few principles are valid without exception. For example, it can be said that men are physically stronger than women and that women are more emotional than men, but there are exceptions to each of these generalizations. It is assumed that the reader, male or female, will not discount the validity of the fundamental principles involved because of individual exceptions.

Perhaps the book's most precarious premise is that anyone, especially a male, knows very much about female behavior or the effective management of women. My defense for this premise is based on some 20 years of experience in interviewing, employing, placing, training, supervising, counseling, discharging, and working with women employees and executives in an organization that includes more than 15,000 females. It is also based on numerous workshops and management seminars I have conducted for both mixed groups and groups composed exclusively of women at all levels of responsibility, locally and internationally; contacts with hundreds of companies and organizations; special research, surveys, and interviews for the purpose of gathering and validating material to be included in this book.

In discussions on the subject of women in both mixed and all-female groups, opinions that differed from my own were welcomed. As a result, most of the material contained in this book has been tested and verified by tryout and feedback as being reasonably accurate and acceptable to both sexes.

It is the intent of this book to be completely objective, to be neither biased for nor against women. However, some men might view the positions taken as profemale and some women might view them as promale. My purpose is to be completely honest in revealing the tremendous potential of women, not because they are perfect or better than men, but because, as individuals, they can produce the results desired. By letting the chips (facts) fall where they will, this book should significantly aid the rapid expansion of woman into all levels of business and management. As expressed by one woman, "We will have to do more and be better leaders in order to take up the slack and fill the gaps being left by men."

The following guides should prove helpful in understanding the book's intent:

The goal is objectivity, prejudiced neither for nor against women.

Statements, opinions, and guides are not true without exception, but are statistically indicative of basic truths.

Points of view or recommendations should not be isolated and judged out of context but in light of the entire book.

Women accept spoken truths about themselves more readily than they do written truths. (Many women have said to me, "What you say is true, but I suppose we just don't like to confront it in writing. We are even willing to hide the good in order to keep the negative from becoming too visible.")

Although the focus here is on women in relation to their work, the insights into understanding and working with them will apply with the same degree of authenticity in the home, in social life, or wherever women are encountered.

Most guides, recommendations, and principles advocated regarding the supervision of women will prove equally valid for supervising men.

Although the term "women" is used at times in a general, all-inclusive sense, I am vividly aware of the wide variation that exists between the inexperienced young girl applying for her first job and the experienced, mature, career woman. Comparable variation exists in job-related areas between the 40-year-old housewife (possibly with limited education), reporting for her first job after rearing a family, and the highly educated, professional woman of the same age who has 20 years of experience and may be a manager.

If the purpose of this book is fulfilled, the result should be increased job-related achievement for both women and men. Also, those concerned (male and female) with women as employees, supervisors, customers, and developers of corporate affairs should be better equipped to cope with female potential and women's contribution to business. It is my firm belief, regarding female potential, that we err more by underestimating than by overestimating the contribution women are capable of making to the human and economic success of an enterprise.

Grateful appreciation is expressed to the thousands of men and women in all levels of business who have contributed to this book.

Ray A. Killian

Contents

part one

Managing the Expanding Influence of Women in Business

Responding to the Female Impact

SHATTERED and destroyed forever are the traditional concepts that a woman's place is in the home, that her role is limited to serving the pleasures and needs of man as sex mate, field hand, household servant, cook, and bearer and guardian of children. She is no longer satisfied to remain placidly at home, no longer content with limited education and unimportant jobs. She has arrived on the business and industrial scene in quantity and is committed to costarring roles with men in every phase of enterprise. The transition has moved her into the factory, the office, the laboratory, and the executive suite as a participant and contributor equal to her male counterpart. Although business has yet to recognize her as man's equal, she insists on two things: a challenge and a chance — a responsible job to be done and an opportunity to do it.

She has come to stay and to produce. She expects opportunities and compensation comparable to a man's. She intends to be heard. She anticipates recognition and personal fulfillment. She expects to work in comfortable and pleasant surroundings. She insists on personal and courteous treatment from her associates and supervisors. She demands facilities appropriate to her special physical and emotional needs. She wants to prove herself a human being who is able to do a job. And she doesn't care that her presence causes changes in traditional practices.

What does she plan to contribute in return? She intends to be dependable, to produce, and to make a profitable contribution to the company in line with the proper matching of her capabilities to her job responsibilities. And she is willing to be judged by the contribution she makes to the goals of the organization. She knows that there is a critical need for capable management with trainable potential in every area of business. She is also painfully aware that the greatest available leadership resource — namely, qualified women — has been virtually untapped.

The next move is up to management. Will distorted judgment and action continue because of past conditions and practices? Or is management willing to follow the enlightened path, filling positions throughout the company with the best qualified people without regard to sex? Will management recognize and benefit from the outstanding promise inherent in womanpower? Will management be willing to make some minor adjustments in supervisory leadership, alterations in employee benefits and the physical environment, and structural changes in the organization in order to obtain her full potential as a contributing and equal member of the team? The survival and growth of the enterprise may realistically depend on the action management takes.

Modern Confrontations with Reality

Both sexes experienced some surprise when they discovered that women now constitute more than one-third of the national workforce; that they are the most available resource for filling the company's critical shortages of personnel; that they are filling the vacuums in managerial positions; that they are becoming technicians, professionals, and scientists.

It should not be surprising that everyone who is concerned with the business world, whether an employer, supervisor, employee, or customer, must be vitally concerned with this female influence. Women must now be considered an integral part of every phase of business activity. To disregard their availability, their presence, their wishes, their power, and their potential is unrealistic and uneconomical. Whenever and wherever either men or women are unwilling to cooperate and work effectively with women, it is because they are not seeing reality as it exists today, and not seeing the obvious trends for the future. Failure to face this reality shortchanges personal self-interests and the interests of the company as well.

The Female Revolution

Is there really a female revolution? Luther Holcomb, vice-chairman of the U.S. Equal Employment Opportunity Commission, stated that women's rights will be as dominant an issue in the seventies as race was in the sixties.

"New wineskins for old" describes the changes occurring in the roles of women in almost every facet of society, especially in the business world. Ingredients for job performance and achievement have become less a matter of physical strength and more a matter of technique, dexterity, and mental skills and their application. Criteria for job success have moved in the direction that favors woman's special talents and interests. The new emphasis on human and social skills is particularly suited to her superiority in these areas. Her opportunities and roles are changing because of:

. . . the significant shifts in the basic nature of job requirements

. . . businesses' critical need for womanpower and its potential contribution

, . . the lessened demands on her time and energies in the home

. . . changes in social mores, which now approve of women — wives and mothers — working outside the home for pay

. . . her increased education and overall qualifications

. . . the concrete evidence that in most job environments she can compete with men on equal terms

. . . the proof that she is capable of making a profitable contribution if appropriately trained, placed, and supervised

. . . women's own resolve to compete with men for leadership positions and benefits [1]

Almost every valid statistical report shows evidence of women's changing roles. "Since 1948, while the male labor force was growing about 7 million, the female force added nearly 14 million to its ranks.[2] Not only has the overall number of working women increased, but women's percentage of the total workforce and their numbers in most job categories have also increased.

A century ago, everything was centered in the home. Husband and wife worked together, usually on a farm, to meet the needs of the family. Today, many activities are being carried on outside the home and the husband-wife circle. Women are moving toward the same type of partnership with men in business as they formerly had on the farm.

[1] *U.S. News & World Report,* April 13, 1970.
[2] *Ibid.*

Women want to do their share, to participate—they are no longer content with a partnership that is limited to their being just half the population and nothing more. Wars, economic influences, changing family status and location, and mass communications have shown women that they are capable of holding positions similar to men's and of competing with men in the business world.

The rapid increase in the number of female college graduates, working wives, working mothers with small children, and females in executive, professional, and a host of other positions indicates dramatically the extent to which woman's roles are undergoing a rapid transition. Both she and the business community are benefiting from these major shifts and changes in society's basic patterns and mores.

In the minds of many people—both men and women—a woman's new status, her new roles, her equality with men, her side-by-side competitiveness with men on the job, her absence from the home, and her assumption of the traditional male role pose possible threats to her once cherished role as being very special and feminine. In the past, men have tended toward one role and women toward a different one. Now, the move is on for women to assume the man's role while, at the same time, retaining her biological role as a woman. Today, being a homemaker is no longer a full-time position that uses women's full potential, nor does being a homemaker provide the identity and fulfillment a woman desires.

The following facts reported by the U.S. Department of Labor are evidence of the changing status and roles of women:

> Girls born in 1900 had a life expectancy of 48 years; by 1967 this had increased to 74 years.
>
> In 1920 only 20 percent of 17-year-old girls were graduated from high school; by 1965 the percentage had increased to 74.
>
> In 1920 only 2 percent of 21-year-old women were graduated from college; by 1965 the figure had increased to 16 percent.
>
> In 1920 only 23 percent of all women aged 14 and over were in the labor force; in 1966 the figure was 39 percent, and it is expected to reach 50 percent by 1980.
>
> In 1920 the average woman worker was single and 28 years old; today the average woman worker is married and 41 years old.
>
> Half of today's women marry by age 21 and have their last child by age 30. By the time the youngest child is in school, the mother may still have 30 to 35 years of active work potential left.
>
> There were 31.1 million women in the labor force as of 1970; this number is expected to increase to 36 million by 1980.

More than one out of every three workers is a woman.

Almost three out of five working women are married and living with their husbands.

Labor-saving household equipment and prepared foods shorten the time required for domestic chores, thus freeing women for other activities.

This almost complete statistical change since World War I is evidence of the deeper change taking place in the private lives of women and in their relationships with those who have contact with them at home, in educational institutions, businesses, or society in general. And, indeed, the logical conclusion is that women have a decisive impact on the basic structure of the cultural and economic functions of these fundamental systems. The real challenge during this upheaval, to both men and women, is to preserve traditional values that are worthwhile, to discard those that are antiquated, and to move boldly into a new world of enlightenment and promise for both sexes.

Women Make Their Presence Felt

It's true that the corporate institution will never be the same again now that such vast numbers of women have entered the business world. And in most instances, the changes that occur are progressive — improving the work environment and increasing profitability. The attitude of fear, or at least of anxiety, on the part of management concerning women's arrival has been replaced by gratitude for their maturity, understanding, dependability, and overall contribution.

Women have made their presence felt in an endless variety of ways. Work benches have been adjusted in height and designed to correspond to a woman's size and contour. Colors are being selected with her preferences in mind. The temperature is set at her comfort level. The convenience and appearance of parking lots are responsive to her safety and peace of mind. Benefits such as hospitalization, vacations, sick leave, maternity leave, and retirement have been restructured to meet her special needs. Safety rules and equipment have been redesigned to meet her esthetic requirements as well as for accident prevention. Rest rooms, lounges, machines, and a host of other facilities have undergone changes that reflect her presence and special preferences.

Her presence has also been felt by supervisors and managers as they have had to shift from supervising an all-male staff to one that is mixed or, in many instances, all female. During a citywide training

session for supervisors, the subject of managing women was discussed. One veteran supervisor remarked that in the production plant
where he worked, the workforce had shifted from all male to all female
in less than ten years. In fact, he stated, he had 140 women under his
direct supervision. At this point, the other members of the group began
to sympathize with him, and he agreed that he deserved their sympathy
— that it was a little rough on him at times. Then a member of the group
asked, "How has this affected production?" The answer was, "It has
improved. We have, of course, made some changes in the machines
being used and in our methods. But I have to admit that the cost of
production has gone down and that the company is very pleased with
the results in the whole department." At this point someone remarked
rather pointedly, "Well, isn't that the name of the game? It seems to me
that the most important thing is results — and these have improved. And
the 'ordeal' hasn't turned your hair gray or caused you to have a heart
attack."

Richest Underutilized Resource

Former Vice-President Hubert H. Humphrey once stated that
women are an underprivileged majority, the so-called weaker sex. But
he added, "One of the richest under-utilized resources in America is
the talent of its women. And this nation has for many years squandered
this talent in shameful fashion." In 1970, more than 64 percent of the
women in the labor force were employed in clerical, service, and sales
positions. The consensus is clear and irrefutable: Today's better-
educated women are ready, capable, and available to assume larger and
more important business roles. The increasing shortage of men in
most areas, including management positions, and the legal requirements of the equal pay and civil rights acts combine to make the inevitable course of action clear. Those in the decision-making drivers'
seats have both a unique opportunity and a responsibility to fully
utilize women's untapped potential.

There are good reasons for management to employ women, to
place them in the most suitable jobs, to give them the most appropriate
training, and to provide the leadership that will convert their potential
into meaningful contributions. However, the successful utilization of
women in the workforce depends largely on the willingness and effectiveness of corporate leadership to create and maintain an environment
that is conducive to reaching that goal.

LEGAL IMPACT ON MANAGING WOMANPOWER

Several hundred years ago, Dr. Samuel Johnson stated an opinion that was shared by many when he said, "Nature has given women so much power that the law very wisely has given them very little." However, since the passage of the first state minimum-wage law and other employee-related acts just prior to World War I, employers have had to be concerned with complying with the law in the employment of women. The most significant regulations affecting women have been passed by the U.S. Congress. They deal with minimum hourly wage rates and overtime pay, equal pay for equal work, and the antidiscrimination requirements of the Civil Rights Act of 1964. Company practices regarding women must now adhere to federal, state, and local laws in addition to the profit-oriented interests of the business.

Fair Labor Standards Act and Amendments

The Fair Labor Standards Act of 1938 established minimum hourly rates and the number of hours beyond which premium rates were required. Regulations in the form of presidential directives established additional minimums and regulatory policies for all government employees and government subcontractors. Amendments to the Fair Labor Standards Act during the 1960s extended the provisions of this law to include a far greater segment of the industrial community and to much smaller companies. This amendment, in conjunction with state laws, brought most employees under the minimum wage and overtime provisions of the law. In most instances, these laws were intended to apply to women.

Equal Pay for Equal Work

Although companies began paying minimum wages and overtime rates to all employees, they were not paying women rates comparable to those they paid men for the same level of responsibility and job performance. U.S. Secretary of Labor Arthur J. Goldberg reported in a letter to President Kennedy in 1961 that the average annual earnings of working women were only three-fifths those of men.

An amendment to the Fair Labor Standards Act, which became effective June 10, 1964, provided that unequal compensation practices be eliminated by requiring that men and women who perform substantially the same job be paid on the same basis. The following excerpt from this law makes the legal impact explicit:

> No employer . . . shall discriminate, within any establishment in which covered employees are employed, between employees on the basis of sex by paying wages to employees in such establishment at a rate less than the rate at which he pays wages to employees of the op- posite sex in such establishment for equal work on jobs the perfor- mance of which requires *equal skill, effort,* and *responsibility,* and which are *performed under similar working conditions,* except where such payment is made pursuant to (1) a seniority system; (2) a merit system; (3) a system which measures earnings by quantity or quality of production; or (4) a differential based on any other factor than sex; provided that an employer who is paying a wage rate differential in violation of this section shall not, in order to comply with the pro- visions of this subsection, reduce the wage rate of any employee.

Interpretation of the law reveals that the basis of pay was intended to include hourly rates, piece rates, commission rates, and all other forms of compensation. The equal pay requirement was intended to include jobs that were basically the same—they did not have to be identical, or exactly the same, to be covered by the law. Thus the fringes or minor functions of the job did not invalidate the equal-pay and equal-treat- ment requirement. The same basic executive and administrative exemptions apply to this law as those in the Fair Labor Standards Act.

Title VII of the Civil Rights Act

On the day the U.S. House of Representatives was scheduled to vote on the Civil Rights Bill of 1964, Congressman Howard K. Smith of Virginia proposed an addition that consisted of one word: sex. Although he introduced this addition rather facetiously and for the purpose of delaying or defeating the bill, it turned out to be a shocker. Smith argued "seriously" for the amendment by pointing out that Title VII was drafted to extend the promise of equal opportunity to 7 million Negroes and that his proposal would include some 25 million working women. Congressman Smith stated that white men earned a median income of $6,497; Negro men, $4,285; white women, $3,859; and Negro women, $2,674.

The entire bill was passed, including the sex amendment (politically astute congressmen were aware of the large number of women voters). Thus, federal law that prohibited discrimination in employment, promo- tion, compensation, discharge, and all other conditions of employment was extended to prohibit discrimination because of race, creed, color, national origin, and, the surprise addition, *sex*. Although a "sleeper," the sex addition immediately affected almost three times as many employees and employers as were affected by the provision regarding the minority groups for whom the bill was originally intended. Employers suddenly had to reexamine their employment, promotion, compensation, discharge, benefits, and other conditions-of-employment practices to make certain that they did not discriminate on the basis of sex.

Thus, the equal-pay law and the law against discrimination because of sex caused management to ask, "Is there any reason why jobs traditionally open to men only cannot be filled by women?" A special survey (see Appendix A for details) indicates that in spite of the law, both men and women know that equality for women does not exist although equal jobs and responsibilities for women have proved to be economically profitable for business.

State and Local Regulations

In addition to federal laws and regulations, most states have their own laws regarding the employment and treatment of women workers. The most significant ones relate to number of hours of work, night work, employment of minors, industrial homework, employment before and after childbirth, occupational limitations (hazardous jobs or weight-lifting limitations), and equal opportunity for women. The federal law and its interpretation makes clear that requirements or restrictions imposed by state laws cannot be used to invalidate any part of the federal requirement. For example, a state law limiting the employment of women to a maximum of 8 hours a day and 48 hours a week could not be used as justification for refusing to employ women or for paying them a lower wage rate because they could not work as many hours a day as men.

Impact of Government Regulations

Every employer covered by the government regulations is required to know and follow all federal, state, and local regulations regarding the employment or conditions of employment of women. The federal wage-hour and equal-pay laws do not at present extend coverage to small businesses, and Title VII of the Civil Rights Act has not extended coverage to companies that employ fewer than 25 people. The wage-hour and equal-pay laws also provide certain exemptions for executives and administrators. But the exemptions and noncoverage provisions are largely illusory since the public is not aware of these exceptions and, therefore, expects all employers to follow the laws as they are generally understood. Perhaps an even stronger reason for businesses not covered by government regulations to abide by the regulations is that they must compete for employees in the same labor market as businesses that are covered. And, in most instances, legal requirements regarding pay rates and conditions of employment concerning women will have to be met or exceeded in order for a company to remain competitive.

HER OPPORTUNITY GROWS AND MANAGEMENT RESPONDS

Doors are now opening, but how do women view this? Management's interests are economic, objective, and legal. Women's interests might be emotional, intuitive, and personal. These different points of view are bound to create difficulties. Management is frequently inclined to regard women as unresponsive to the economic needs of the enterprise; and women are likely to feel that business is insensitive to their personal needs and desires.

If a woman is realistic, she knows that her acceptance and placement in certain jobs are often given reluctantly and with fingers crossed. She suspects that if management had enough men available and if there were no laws to protect her, she would not be able to get desirable jobs. Psychologically she must wrestle with the conscious or subconscious knowledge that she is second choice. She has some justifiable uncertainties about her abilities, about leaving her family during the day, and about her success on the job. And knowing that she is often less than welcome adds to her anxiety. If management is to make the goals of the enterprise compatible with those of its female employees, it must understand their point of view, their thinking, and their desires regarding the company, as well as their reactions to the industrial environment.

Mushrooming Opportunities for Women

Even more significant than the large number of women entering business are the kinds of jobs that are being made available to them. Despite the resistance women have received when placed in leadership positions, they have moved steadily forward in their quest for equality of opportunity and responsibility.

Because of the legal prohibitions against discrimination and the desperate need for human resources, women can now embark on educational pursuits and training programs that will qualify them for positions which were previously unavailable to them. They can now apply for any job that appeals to them or for one where the company will train them.

Between 1950 and 1960 the number of female managers tripled; and since that time, the growth rate has been even greater. As industry's need for specially skilled, technical, educated, and managerial talent increases, and as women's aspirations expand, more women will aim for — and get — a preferred spot on the management team. Perhaps the key to a woman's expanded opportunities is the fact that she will be able to play a vital management role on the first team instead of being relegated to a supporting one. The problem of identifying and responding to this increased opportunity is emphasized in the following statement by the board chairman of a consumer goods manufacturing company:

> My premise is that woman conceives her role to be that of helper to an individual — as mother, wife, secretary. To succeed in management, she must substitute for this limited image of herself a vision of her job as potentially helpful to whole segments of society.[3]

In order for women to take advantage of the ever increasing number of opportunities open to them, they are moving from a one-to-one relationship into positions of leadership that can contribute to the whole corporation and to all of society. Women's growing awareness of their own potential is enabling them to move into completely new areas with a full measure of self-confidence and a willingness to compete on an equal basis with their male counterparts. Many executives tend to believe that today the principal limitation to female opportunity is not prejudice against women, but the limited availability of women with the necessary educational, technical, and motivational qualifications for available openings.

A woman executive who supervises 30 women said that women's biggest obstacle in their search for equal status, compensation, and positions in the business world is their lack of self-confidence so that, in essence, they are defeating themselves while striving to attain their goal.

[3] Garda W. Bowman, et al., "Are Women Executives People?" *Harvard Business Review* (July–August 1965), p. 14.

Suspended in an Environment of Change

Women have experienced prejudice and hostility on the business scene. They have been subjected to ridicule and skepticism. They have played second fiddle and waited patiently, if not always passively, for an opportunity to prove their equal competence with men.

Although the business environment is rapidly changing, it still does not offer conditions of complete equality. But the trend is clear. There is less prejudice every day against women's presence on the job, more willingness to judge them objectively, and an increased tendency to both compensate and promote them in accordance with their abilities. However, those who still lack confidence in female employees and supervisors and who continue to treat women unfairly deserve serious management attention. It is only through the understanding of women's problems, values, and reactions to change, as well as through appropriate recognition of their efforts, that a supervisor, male or female, will be able to use effectively the full potential of womanpower. It is for these reasons that considerable space in this book is devoted to the causes of these conditions, to current practices, and to specific recommendations for their correction.

Assessing Women's Influence

It is highly doubtful that most members of both sexes have yet recognized the full impact of woman's influence on all future business decisions and activity. It is obvious that women's presence in business must inevitably affect the operation of the business and the processes of management. Women's availability and influence provide new human resources, new talent for leadership, new technicians for our automated world, and new possibilities for meeting the challenge of the knowledge explosion.

Automation and computers have had a dramatic effect on corporate structure. No less dramatic has been the influence of the twentieth-century woman on corporate structure as she has moved her base of operation from the home and farm to the factory, office, financial institution, marketplace, and executive suite.

Women have entered the man-made, man-controlled business world, and this male-dominated structure is now assuming new shapes and characteristics that have an obvious feminine influence. We are becoming aware of the female's positive role in mankind's climb to a higher standard of living, improved human values, and the more realistic and equitable use of all human resources.

Unfortunately, not all negative attitudes have been eliminated, but women are proving themselves: They are competing, they are performing successfully, and they are achieving their objectives.

Women are not perfect, but then, neither are men. However, they have repeatedly exhibited their competence and their potential. The wisest management course is to take women into full partnership in the plant, the bank, and the executive office. Women, in turn, will generously reward the individual, the business, and the economy. They will add to the personal fulfillment of everyone concerned through the trust placed in them.

2

Understanding Women

THROUGHOUT history men have found women to be mysterious. When a male manager throws up his hands and laments that women are impossible to understand, he is abdicating both his human and his managerial responsibilities. Women may have different drives, motivations, interests, needs, and demands from those of men, but these differences are certainly not incomprehensible. And if a manager wants an effective, harmonious working team, he must be willing to try to understand the women who work for him.

Penetrating the Feminine Mystique

Psychologists and educators contend that there is very little difference between men and women, although differences obviously do exist. However, few men recognize that the differences are small, and they are, therefore, filled with anxieties when they try to understand women.

Yet in spite of all the difficulties that might be encountered on the way to understanding both women and men, the establishment and maintenance of effective working relationships must be achieved as a basis for daily job effectiveness. It is hoped that a sharper focus on certain female characteristics and the identification of female behavior patterns will aid in penetrating the so-called feminine mystique.

When a man looks intently into the crystal ball in hopes that it will give him a clearly focused picture of women, he sees instead a fuzzy, befogged, and distorted image. He experiences a feeling of inadequacy as he tries to adjust the focus and gain sharper perception. Yet his efforts continue to prove futile until he realizes that the distortion is not in the image but in the lens of his own limited mental vision. His understanding is circumscribed by his own experience, most of which has been in a male-oriented and male-shaped world. It has consisted of being a son, brother, father, pursuer, athletic superior, and the dominating male at work.

As the male attempts to understand and supervise the working woman, he is met with a completely new set of conditions and responses. He must look through the lenses of the other sex: the sister, the daughter, the mother, and the new arrival on the industrial scene. As he endeavors to reach a rapport with women, he is forced to consider new influences, different reactions to the same set of stimuli, and different psychological drives. When he discovers that his established basis for making value judgments and decisions is not completely valid where women are concerned, he is puzzled, confused, and critical. Reluctantly he concludes that he must alter his thinking before he can even begin to understand women.

Keys to Her Predictability

If there is a key to understanding human behavior, especially female behavior, it is the ability to predict reactions. The whole structure of successful relationships with working women rests solidly on this foundation of predictability. It has been alleged many times that women are not predictable — but women *are* predictable. This is the only basis on which to construct present relationships and to influence future courses of action. True, women might exhibit more extremes of emotion, might be more vocal and demonstrative in expressing their feelings, and might be more likely to have greater influence on both women and men, but still they are predictable and conform to statistical norms. Practical guides on influencing and predicting behavior are valid when based on these key factors:

An acceptance of the principle of cause-and-effect relationships. Behavior and reaction are caused; influence on cause means influence on result.

A clear concept of the reactions and behavior patterns needed to achieve expected results.

An understanding of psychological drives and responses, including female and individual differences.

An awareness of what influences will be necessary to cause the desired reactions to occur.

Knowledge and understanding of which current causes and resultant responses are likely to occur.

Sufficient persuasive leadership techniques to produce the desired behavior.

This approach is not a premeditated manipulation of people or a calculated design to make puppets of others. Rather, it is the factual recognition of the consistency and predictability of human behavior. In our day-to-day relationships with women, we are constantly confronted with the need for favorable reactions to our leadership activities or courses of action. The principle of predictability merely recognizes that reactions and future behavior can be forecast. Once we know the past behavior patterns of a group or an individual and the future patterns we want, we can select stimuli that will most likely cause the desired behavior which will in turn lead to the desired goals. For example, courtesy will elicit a more favorable reaction than rudeness; genuine concern and interest in a person will create more rapport than will disinterest; subordinates who trust their supervisor will react more favorably to him than if they distrust him; employees who are adequately trained and motivated are more likely to perform satisfactorily than those without such training and motivation.

Awareness of the predictability principle should eliminate most surprises and unexpected disappointments. If a supervisor abides by the laws governing human relationships, he will have fewer negative and strained associations. In most instances, the reactions and attitudes that we elicit from others are predictable because they are responses engendered by our own behavior and influence.

This predictability principle becomes the key to understanding and projecting the reactions and behavior of women. It reveals to us, whether male or female, the types of relationships and leadership that must be provided in order to insure favorable reactions and responses. The crux of this formula then leads to practical understanding of female behavior, past, present, and future. What is its nature? How is it changing? Can it be understood? What is necessary in order to create favorable relationships? How can women's potential best be tapped and used to the benefit of all concerned? Penetrating more fully into this "feminine mystique" is an attempt to establish the foundation of knowledge on which to build favorable relationships and to channel potential contributions.

In spite of the valid justification for predictability, there are still some unpredictable mavericks in the group. When one makes the statement that women are less predictable than men, exceptions are always raised. If it is casually mentioned that both women and men prefer male supervisors, again individual exceptions are cited. After all, in most statistical distributions a few individuals will not adhere to the norm. But the majority will, and it is this majority that makes up the predictable patterns of behavior.

Most of the statements and opinions expressed in this book regarding women, and the differences between them and men, are true for most women most of the time, since we are looking for the best and most practical ways to work with most women most of the time. The particular focus here is on the degree and range of variations in the predictability of women.

Women Can Be Understood

It's true that women can be understood, supervised, and directed toward business-oriented goals and activities. Although men may never think of women as anything but mysterious and enigmatic, the consistency of women's reactions and behavior will eventually lead men to the conclusion that women can be understood and that they can be as easy or as difficult to work with as men.

To be successful, a supervisor must be able to forecast job activity, attitudes, reactions, and results. He must base his forecasting on his knowledge of human behavior in general as well as on his knowledge of specific people. For example, women employees involved in production or piecework would require a different kind of supervision from those in management positions, regardless of the fact that women in both jobs have the same basic female characteristics. Leadership ability should cause him to exert the specific kind of influence that will bring about the desired job performance and minimize undesirable qualities.

The importance of this emerges when the executive recognizes that in order to achieve certain established goals, specific job activities must be performed. It follows, then, that his knowledge of women should give him the assurance that he is the influence that can cause the desired behavior or performance. His skill in predicting feminine behavior can create the environment that will lead to the desired activity. The most significant ingredient in this mix is not so much the external environment as the personal climate and interpersonal relationships that evoke response and effort. The woman is more dependent on inner feelings or drives than on overt activities.

The individual woman (like the individual man) cannot be understood as a complex whole. She reacts to specific areas of human activity. A consideration of the following areas should increase the practical understanding of women's behavior on the job:

Playing the roles expected. All their lives, many men and women have had roles that were distinctly different from each other. Each subconsciously perpetuates the role perceived to be characteristic of his or her sex. An awareness of these expected roles can aid in the understanding of apparent female differences.

Her search for identity and meaning. A man's primary reason for working is the support of his family. It is reasonable to assume, therefore, that he is motivated (more than women) to make more money, increase his job security, and seek promotions. In contrast, many women want something different from their job. A woman has an economic interest and a concern for promotions and job security (identical to those of men), but these may not be her primary reasons for working. If she comes from a middle- to higher-income family, she is probably working to get away from the routine of unchallenging housework into a more stimulating environment. The woman who is working for personal fulfillment, to give meaning to her life, and to identify with the excitement of business brings a different outlook to her job. It is a challenge for her supervisor to understand what stimulates her, and how to motivate her.

Her reactions to competing with men. Up to this point, men have had to compete with other men, but seldom have they had to compete with women for status on the corporate totem pole. Women are, likewise, accustomed to competing with other women. But when they arrive in the business world, they not only have to compete with women, but they also have to compete with men — and often with men who might be less intelligent and less qualified than they.

Her inexperience on the business scene. Since women are relatively new to the business world, they are obviously less experienced than men in corporate operations. The woman who has never worked before has to feel her way until she reaches the same level of corporate maturity as a man. (Obviously this does not apply to the experienced career woman.)

The critical element in business success is still a human one, despite sophisticated automation, electronic data processing (EDP), and electronic communication. As compared with the complexities of employing, training, motivating, and supervising women, machines are relatively easy to cope with. Yet it is precisely the supervisor's responsibility to deal with women on the job, and he can cope with all the problems involved only if he recognizes and follows available basic guides.

It has been demonstrated that almost any supervisor of normal intelligence and a sincere desire to be an effective manager can acquire considerable skill in the art of working with women, provided he is responsive to the known facts and applies them thoughtfully, conscientiously, and persistently. History, literature, psychology, personal experience, and special studies are all vital resources to consider and evaluate. Women's historical patterns of behavior and reactions and the demands they are now voicing supply the best information for supervisors. Understanding must be based not on conjectures or theories, but on distilled facts.

The title on an article in a business publication posed the question, "Want to Succeed in Business? Then Learn More About Women." It is possible to master the fundamentals of EDP, economics, production, financing, and marketing and still fail in the most vital management areas unless the skills of knowing and managing women are also learned and practiced. The most difficult aspect of leadership is that results must be achieved through others. And in business today, a large percentage of these results depend on the work performed by women.

If a supervisor wishes to be a success, he will get to know women better, and he will work to improve results by availing himself of their abilities and potential. This is a positive move toward the best utilization of womanpower and will lead to the achievement of set goals. Once the supervisor realizes that his success depends on the abilities of his women employees, he will stop resenting their presence on the job and start helping them achieve their full potential.

3

Women's Differences, Roles, and Expectations

THERE are significant differences between men and women beyond the obvious physical ones. These differences can affect both job performance and the techniques used by supervisors to manage women. Some of these differences can be advantages, while others may have potentially negative effects. Management's challenge then is to identify these differences and to make the best use of them.

As women form a larger portion of the workforce, their presence should be viewed not as an added problem but as a welcome solution to problems. One wise executive summed it up with the statement, "Women are different, but that doesn't mean difficult. A supervisor will not do a good job if he is intimidated by the mistaken idea that women are impossibly sensitive and temperamental." When the differences are identified, evaluated in proper perspective, and considered in light of the requirements of the job, women usually measure up favorably. The key is to view these differences in relation to the job. A manager should not view an employee as a problem just because that employee is a woman.

A Battle of the Sexes?

When a woman enters the business world, she is, perhaps for the first time, in a position of having to compete with men. And she must be prepared to compete on their terms. But some women use their feminine wiles to make the going a little easier for themselves, and this, unfortunately, adds to the uncertainties, frustrations, and fears men feel about women on the job. It is painful for a man to lose a job or promotion to another man; but the possibility of losing it to a woman is a gnawing threat and possible source of embarrassment.

The following paragraphs state the differences between men and women that might influence women's job performance and their supervision.

Women are more subjective and intuitive.

Men have always been the achievers in business. For this reason, women have had to take a back seat or have had to use more initiative, show greater intelligence, and work harder to prove themselves.

Women are more sensitive and are more likely to take things personally. A woman might take criticism of her work as criticism of herself. On the other hand, her heightened sensitivity may make her more responsive to the feelings of others. This "supersensitivity" is what we call woman's intuition. According to Dr. George W. Crane, this intuition has been acquired through a close study of their human environment beginning with the family and continuing on the job. It has been to women's advantage to detect slight changes in the tone and expression of their male associates. The social custom that permits a woman less initiative in choosing her male friends has compelled her to become more skilled in stratagems and tact. After years of operating in this way, she forms opinions on such small stimuli that it is not always possible to translate the "intuition" into objective symbols and communicative logic.[1]

Women have been put on the defensive and feel that they must constantly prove themselves.

When women are taken for granted or ignored, they assume they are being disapproved of.

Women need and expect more praise.

Women are more interested in people than in things.

Women like to talk more. Because of this, they usually do better work in a group than they do when they are isolated.

Working conditions are often more important to women than money.

Women are quicker to spot favoritism or preferential treatment.

Most women (particularly those who have never worked before) need more orientation and initial job training.

---

[1] George W. Crane, *Psychology Applied* (Chicago: Hopkins Syndicate, Inc., 1946), p. 145.

A study of the vocational interests of women and men at Stanford University concluded that women and men have equal intelligence, but that because their interests are different, men appear to be smarter in business.[2]

Men have traditionally displayed a greater interest in mechanics, scientific activities, and physical pursuits and in legal, political, sales, military, and financial activities. Women have traditionally been more interested in literature, people, clerical work, teaching, social work, merchandising, and fashion. (It's possible that women's interests are so different from those of men because women have been excluded from the man's world for so long.)

Women are more concerned with associates, friends, the quality of supervision, and the surroundings of a job, whereas men are more interested in the benefits, opportunities for advancement, and the salary a job has to offer.

Women judge jobs in terms of immediate satisfaction, whereas men look at jobs with a longer-range point of view.

Because many women are wives, mothers, and managers of homes, as well as workers, a greater percentage of a woman's time and her physical, mental, and emotional resources are concentrated in the home. Therefore, women find work less important and less fulfilling than men. More of men's energies are exerted in their jobs. And, since women are more involved in their home life, they are more likely to bring their problems to work.

Women are biologically different from men. The average woman is about half as strong as the average man. Even large women are not as strong as small men. Women's general physical makeup is not well suited for heavy work and long, unbroken periods of physical activity. And every month women react to stimuli the male body never experiences.

Women are usually more emotional than men, and their emotional reactions are quicker. This causes stronger attachments to social relationships on the job and quicker responses to the demands of the job. And they tend to express their feelings more openly than men.

Women are more socially oriented. They have a greater need for social acceptance, recognition, and other people's approval.

Many women are well suited for using precision tools, inspecting products, typing, and assembling small or intricate components. They generally possess a better sense of color than men. They have more

[2] Edgar S. Ellman, *Managing Women in Business* (Waterford, Conn.: National Foreman's Institute, 1967).

patience and adjust better to routine work—and they will stay with it longer than men. They are willing to give more attention to small details and exacting work.

Women's reasons for working may be different from those of men. Some women may be working only temporarily—until their child has completed college or whatever—while men consider working the permanent state of affairs.

Responding to Her Differences

What effects do women's differences have on job performance, supervision, and company activities? A woman may not be as strong physically as a man; she may be more social and want different things from her job; she may think differently and want a different kind of supervision; or she may expect to work a shorter period of time. But these things do not necessarily make her a less productive or less valuable employee. With modern technology making fewer physical demands on the job and with appropriate management leadership, most of her differences can be used to the advantage of the company. As a matter of fact, many of her differences are distinct assets in the more modern and progressive companies where new demands for adroitness in human relations are replacing the need for muscle.

Regardless of the differences that exist between men and women, each woman is an individual, acts as an individual, and wants to be treated as an individual. And she deserves to be approached and supervised as an individual.

THE CHALLENGE OF HER MANY ROLES

A working man has two loyalties—his home and his job. But he often concentrates more on his job since it is his one claim to status and purpose. Not so with a wife and mother. Her first loyalty is to her husband, her children, and her home. Whatever time she has left, she is willing to devote to a job. But, if she has to make a choice between the two, she usually makes it in favor of the home. Obviously, the greatest time demands are on working widows, divorcées, and mothers with children still at home. Wives without children have fewer demands, and single women often experience no greater demands than men. The strength of the demand on a mother's time is significantly influenced by the age and number of her children, the amount of assistance with home duties she receives from domestic help or from older children, and the extent to which her husband shares in the overall responsibilities of running the home.

Who Are the Working Women?

The composition of the female work group has radically changed regarding marital status, educational background, and age. Knowing who the working women are is important to their successful job adjustment and supervision. A mature, married woman in her fifties is not likely to require the same amount or kind of supervision as an energetic 18-year-old just out of high school. The ambitious, career-minded bachelor woman, age 40, responds differently and has different job-related needs from the widow who is working to support three children.

Following are some facts about the female work group as of 1969:

Almost 17 million wives, whose husbands are present in the home, are currently working.

In more than one-third of the husband-wife families, the wife brings home a pay check.

More than 45 percent of wives are working to supplement a family income of less than $7,000 a year.

One-third of all mothers with children under the age of six work.

The more education a woman has, the more likely she is to be working.

The unemployment rate for women is almost double that of men, and women average only three-fifths as much salary.

Nearly half of all women between the ages of 18 and 64 work at least part time during each month.

It is often the wife's income, though smaller than the husband's, that raises the family income above the poverty level.

The greater the family income, the greater the likelihood that the wife is working. However, this percentage declines above the $15,000 income level.

Four out of five working mothers have a husband present in the home.

More than half the 5 million women who are heads of households work outside the home.

The presence of female relatives (grandmothers, aunts, and such) in the home makes it more likely that the mother with young children will work.

Approximately half the women who work outside the home do not have to. Their families could survive without the extra income although they would not live as comfortably.

What is the profile of the typical working woman? She is in her early forties, married, a mother, reasonably well educated, and working primarily for economic reasons. Although this is the statistical picture, remember that each woman is an individual and must be treated as such. But it is important for the supervisor to know that women employees are more likely to be married mothers, rather than young single people or career women.

To Work or Not to Work?

The typical woman is dedicated to her family and home. But she recognizes that one way of serving her family is by earning additional money. If she is a married mother, the final work decision is usually based on her own particular family circumstances: attitudes and wishes of husband and children, severity of economic need, availability of child care, and ultimately, her desire to work and her confidence in her ability to perform two jobs.

But at the time the decision is made—and possibly throughout her working career—she might continue to experience doubts, feel that her husband would prefer her to stay home, and wonder whether her children need her at home and whether her presence there would have prevented any of their problems. She wonders whether extra money— there might not be much after taxes and the additional expenses—is really worth the sacrifice. And she will be plagued by statements such as, "A woman can't be outstanding both at home and in business. She has to make a choice." "It is hard to stay happily married while working." "The quality of motherhood will suffer when the mother works full time."

Although many women, and many men as well, would disagree with statements like these, it is certainly true that strong demands are placed on working women. However, the challenge can be and is being met successfully; supervisors of working women require a little extra patience, understanding, and assistance.

Resolving Her Conflicts

The working woman who must fill two major roles and who expects to be effective in both must find ways to resolve conflicts when they arise. As long as she tries to exist in a state of conflict, she is likely to be unsuccessful in what she seeks to achieve in both worlds.

The keys to her remaining happily married and gainfully employed are the degree of understanding she receives at home and her self-discipline in carrying out her responsibilities in both areas. A company may find it beneficial to provide special assistance for women who are easing their way into the business world for the first time, in case they need guidance in solving certain personal problems, transportation problems, and making the transition from housewife to employee in a highly structured job environment.

EXPECTATIONS: HIS AND HERS

What do the men (husband and supervisor) in a woman's life expect of her in connection with her work? What does she expect of herself? What does the company expect of her? Does the company or her supervisor assume that her job performance will be different from a man's simply because she is a woman?

If a woman is realistic, she knows that she is entering a man's world, where she is outnumbered and outranked by men. This world's size, shapes, and standards are of male origin — they were designed for male needs, strengths, and preferences. Everything is new and strange to her, so it is not to her discredit that it might take her longer than a man to adjust. It is to her credit that she does adjust; she learns the ropes with amazing adeptness and is soon contributing substantially to the company.

His Expectations of Her

Occasionally, male supervisors want to be mothered and comforted by their women subordinates. Sometimes they seek "daughters" whom they can safely boss. But a supervisor's expectations of women and men should be basically the same in regard to meeting the requirements of the job. Men have no right to expect social partners on the job; and although women have a right to be treated with dignity, they should not expect to be catered to.

The expectations of individual supervisors and company management become extremely important in the employment of women. Not surprisingly, people have a knack for finding in others what they expect to find. If the male supervisor expects the working woman to be temperamental, he will probably find her temperamental. If he suspects that she really should not be in the business world, he will often, either consciously or unconsciously, attempt to prove the validity of his conviction.

The prudent supervisor expects and requires the same contribution from women and men. And he structures the requirements of the job, the performance standards, and related influences accordingly.

What She Expects of Herself

Women tend to sell themselves short. They need higher goals and better personal adjustment in order to progress on the job. Whether because of tradition, repeated disappointments, or actual company limitations, women's expectations of themselves and what they can do on the job are often too low. This might seem surprising in view of women's constant struggle for equal opportunity for jobs and promotions. But her newness in the world of business and her unfamiliarity with it, the demands on her time at home, her conditioned inclination to accept leadership from men, and her uncertain tenure of employment often combine to lower her self-esteem. However, the supervisor can substantially strengthen her self-image through recognition, reassurance, praise, and overt efforts to increase her self-confidence.

What she expects from the job often relates directly to her reasons for working. The fulfillment of these expectations controls her response and job commitment. Her principal reasons are contained in the following eight statements:

1. According to the U.S. Department of Labor, most women work because they need the money they earn.

2. Age and marital status often determine a woman's reasons for working. Young women often work just until they get married. They are looking for immediate benefits and glamour. Young single women are not as interested in benefits as in what the job offers on a short-range basis. Married women or heads of households who are trying to keep the family together are not as interested in benefits as in salary. Women over 45 often shift their interest from pay to security benefits: They seek employment for social security coverage, company insurance and hospitalization, and other employee benefits.

3. Many women entered the business world and remained in it simply because their contribution was needed. During World War II, millions of women accepted full-time employment because of the critical shortage of men and the need for increased production. And once they adjusted to the work routine and the advantages of extra income, many continued to work after the end of the war or returned to the job market within a few years.

4. A sizable number of women in their thirties and forties who seek full-time employment for the first time are in search of additional income to provide extras for the family and improve their standard of

living. Scores of job applicants have been known to say, "I haven't worked away from home since I got married 20 years ago. But we decided that my husband's salary just isn't enough to cover our son's college expenses. My working seems to be the only way to pay for his education." It is also her extra income that pays for the furniture, the second car, the family vacation, a child's summer camp, and the dental bills. Most women who enter the business world to meet a specific need continue to work after that need has been met, because they have developed the habit of working, and other needs can always arise.

5. Still other women want to participate in interesting and challenging activities in the business world. They enjoy meeting people and believe that they will be living a more useful life. Women are now better educated and have fewer demands on their time at home. They are promised opportunities and salaries equal to a man's and they want a piece of the action. They grow bored staying home, especially when their children are grown and have left. Working makes a woman feel that she is still needed and that she is making a useful contribution. Marriage and motherhood, at any stage, offer many satisfactions, but not enough to tap the complete resources of multidimensional human beings. Emily H. Mudd identifies the problem in this way:

> The modern American woman is a curious paradox; she has almost everything that thoughtful and intelligent women have wanted and lacked for many centuries, yet there are many indications that she is not really content with herself or her place in contemporary life. The emancipated middle-class American woman—free to train her mind and use it, free to move about unchaperoned in her society, free to marry for personal joy—is more nearly a complete human being than any Western woman since the days of the Roman Empire. Yet far from being completed and fulfilled by all of this, it appears that she is often unsure of what to do with her freedoms, distracted and intimidated by her many opportunities, fearful that she may lose her femininity if she experiments too far with them, and fretful, bored, and discontented when she limits herself to safe, traditional ways.[3]

Women ask, "What am I living for?" "Where am I going?" For many, being a nighttime wife, a daytime guardian of children, a cook, and a housekeeper is not enough. A woman is capable of performing challenging tasks and engaging in a wide range of intellectual activities. She wants to be a person, an individual, and a contributor who is not

---

[3] Emily H. Mudd, Foreword to Morton M. Hunt, *Her Infinite Variety* (New York: Harper & Row, 1962).

restricted by traditions; she wants to decide for herself how to use her potential in order to experience personal satisfaction.

6. A few women work in the hope of finding a husband. These might be youngsters just out of high school or college, bachelor girls, widows, or divorcées. Their primary concern is to meet men; they are not necessarily concerned with the long-range benefits of permanent employment.

7. Increasingly, women are seeking the right to choose how they will make their contribution to their family and their community.

8. Also, today many women are better educated and better qualified than ever before. And they are pursuing full-time careers as a matter of choice. They intend to remain employed, are pursuing professional growth, and are successful in combining career and marriage.

Factors That Can Interfere with Her Job Performance

Although a woman has worthwhile qualities that are advantages in the business world, she may also have some qualities or characteristics that can interfere with her full and permanent commitment to the requirements of the job. For example, many women don't have to work. Some women employees have been known to say, "Well, remember that I don't *have* to work. My husband has a good job and can support me. If things don't improve in the department, I'll quit." Men, on the other hand, rarely have wives who are supporting them. This can make a tremendous difference in the amount of dissatisfaction a woman is willing to accept on the job. There are 18 million women who could stop working without destroying their families' standard of living. This makes the average woman less tolerant of things she finds distasteful in her job. And she may be less dedicated to her job, her company, and her supervisor than a man is.

Like men, women are often their own worst enemies in regard to their opportunities and job performance. In survey after survey, both men and women agree that the most serious impediment to the equal treatment of women is the way women act once they are employed. If a woman expects special treatment, a bending of the rules in her favor, or lowered performance standards; and if she won't accept responsibility and resists supervision, she is essentially undermining the basic equality for which she struggles.

part two

Employing and
Using Womanpower

Guides to Recruitment, Employment, and Placement

PEOPLE, and more specifically women, should be employed on the basis of merit. The company—through the job applicants it seeks, its selection tools and processes, and its placement practices—must select the best qualified woman available at the price it can afford to pay.

During World War II, women were the major human resource available. Since that time, they have entered the workforce at twice the rate of men. Today, housewives and mothers constitute the largest pool of unemployed adults, and the employer who has positions to be filled recognizes that he has a better chance of filling them with women than with men.

How Long Will She Work?

Typically, men expect to remain employed from the time they complete their education until normal retirement age. But what about women? The average length of employment for an 18-year-old girl is only 18 months. The more children a woman has, and the later she has her last child, the shorter her expected work life is. Fewer than one-fifth of working women remain on the job more than five years after marriage. Their husbands may be transferred. Emergencies in the home may force a woman to leave her job. She might not have to work and may quit any time certain financial needs have been met. Women are freer than men to change jobs or remain unemployed for indefinite periods of time. Of course, women who never marry have the most continuous and the longest attachment to the workforce.

It's true that women are in the workforce for a shorter period of time than men; and it's true that women have a higher turnover rate than men. However, these factors are not legal justification for refusing to hire women. And, apart from the provisions of the law, women are still the most available and most economically sound human investment the company can make.

RECRUITMENT

Every company must be willing to do as much recruiting as the situation demands. Following are a few of the methods available for finding applicants:

Walk-ins. Women who just walk in (without previous contact) and apply for a job. In most instances, this resource proves insufficient and additional methods must be used.

Private employment agencies. Particularly those that specialize in placing women. When placing job orders, make it clear that the company is willing and anxious to employ women. Be sure to list the specific requirements of the jobs to be filled.

Public employment agencies. State employment security commissions and others.

Classified and display-type ads. Those found in newspapers and trade publications.

Radio and television. Telephone companies, department stores, and other companies employing a large number of women make extensive use of radio and often schedule the announcements at times when the housewife is expected to be listening.

Employee referrals. Present employees can be encouraged to pass the word and refer women applicants to the employment office. Some companies encourage this practice by giving bonuses for each referral that is employed and remains for a specified length of time.

Posters. Those found in grocery stores and other places frequented by women.

High schools, business schools, community and four-year colleges. Those with female graduates.

Fashion publications. Those likely to be read by women.

Transfers within the company. It is especially good psychology to post openings on bulletin boards, thus assuring women of the opportunities for better and different jobs.

Other sources. Former employees, teachers, customers and suppliers, clergymen, personal friends, and social and industrial organizations.

These are but a few of the many methods and resources available for finding and recruiting women. But regardless of the method used, the important point to remember is to choose women-oriented media carefully and to use specific appeals that women will respond to. It should also be remembered that prospective women applicants might be primarily interested in location, working hours, pay, working conditions, and pleasant associates and supervisors. They should be made to understand that the company sincerely wants and needs them. During recruiting, they must be told enough about the company to make them want to work for it. If it is possible to use women on a short-hour schedule during hours convenient for them, say so. Since many women may be unfamiliar with modern business facilities and work schedules, give them as much insight and information as is practical in all the recruiting materials.

Make it easy for women to apply for work. Make the selection procedure just as pleasant and painless as possible. Some steps that can help your recruitment campaign follow.

Take the recruiting office to the women. If a new plant has to be staffed, large numbers of seasonal extras employed, or current openings filled, make the employment office as convenient to women as possible. Why not locate a temporary office in the shopping center, a convenient neighborhood office, or where the greatest number of women will be exposed to it? Also, on company premises, locate the main employment office where it is easy to find—near the entrance. Don't hide it in a warehouse or at the end of a labyrinth of corridors.

Make the office cheerful and inviting. Women who have never worked before will probably approach the employment office with reluctance and anxiety, so it should look cheerful and seem truly inviting. It should be clean, well furnished, and businesslike, as well as colorful and comfortable looking. Most important, it must provide privacy, which is essential. An office with all these qualities will be as appealing to men as to women.

Use the best qualified recruiting personnel. The single most important factor in the whole recruitment and employment procedure is the person who represents the company to the applicant. A large part of the attitudes, impressions, and feelings formed by the applicant about the company are shaped by this person. And, in the final analysis, it is the recruiter's special skills and abilities that make the applicant want to work for the company. Employment personnel should be people with the unique tact and ability to establish immediate rapport with an applicant. The interviewer must be skilled in listening and in interpreting what he hears.

Be flexible. Many women want to, but cannot, work a full eight-hour schedule; others can work only during certain hours. Many companies have been successful in using two women, each working four hours, to fill one full-time job. After all, it's better to have a short-hour person on the job than no one at all. Understanding and flexibility on the part of the company (within certain limits) will attract many women to the workforce.

Make special interview hours. Interview women when they are available for interviews. This might be between 6 P.M. and 9 P.M. Or it might be at lunchtime. Some companies post notices with very restrictive hours for interviewing such as between 9 and 11, and 2 and 4; or interviews on Tuesdays and Thursdays only. Then they wonder why more women don't apply for jobs.

Recruiting efforts, the image of the company, and other factors might have to be specifically structured to meet the particular needs of women. The recruiters who travel outside the company, as well as those who interview within, should also engage in special training in order to make the right appeals.

SELECTION AND EMPLOYMENT

What do you do after the ads have been run or the word has been passed, and women start flocking in to apply for jobs? The interviewers are now faced with the difficult challenge of selecting those women to be employed. The following areas are important in the selection and employment procedure:

Job specifications. The guide for all selection should be the actual requirements of each job or group of reasonably similar jobs. These specifications should be analyzed critically. How long has it been since they were revised? How much have the actual demands of the job changed since the revisions were made? Are they structured to favor men and discriminate against women? (This might be the unintentional result of the past practices of employing only men for this job.) Are certain requirements no longer relevant or valid? It might be wise to restructure the specifications so that women more readily fit the job requirements. Remember that job specifications should serve as a guide; they are not a rigid formula. The interviewer should be able to be flexible, taking into consideration the special aptitudes of women.

Company characteristics. What peculiarities exist in the company's makeup and operation? What philosophy, beliefs, practices, and policies would women have to accept if they are employed? Is there anything in these practices that might impose hardships on women? It has been said that most interviewers, especially operating line executives, are looking for someone in their own image—someone who appears to have the same qualifications and aptitudes as theirs. If such an executive were interviewing women, he might not find their qualifications very acceptable.

Company facilities. The company must provide the facilities required by law and take women's preferences into consideration as well. When placing women in departments or areas for the first time, the company should review the adequacy of its facilities. If, for example, the workforce shifts from largely male to largely female, more rest rooms would have to be installed and lounges might require changes.

Tools for Selection

The purpose of the selection process is to determine the qualifications of the woman, to predict her probable job performance, to evaluate her capacity for growth, and to anticipate her overall adjustment and contribution. Selection tools and techniques should be specifically designed to insure selection of the woman who has the best chance for job success on a particular job with a particular company.

Certain selection tools are designed to be objective, whereas others are purely subjective. Tests, minimum qualification standards, physical examinations, and reference checks attempt to be objective and provide a quantified view of applicants. Interviews, evaluation of the objective results, and overall assessment of the applicant are largely subjective. In the final analysis, the quality and fairness of the selection process depend largely on the skill and judgment of the employment personnel. Even if the company complies with the law and creates favorable public relations, the hiring of the best qualified women hinges largely on the selection processes and the individuals involved. If the interviewers attach too much or too little significance to any facet of an applicant's qualifications, the effectiveness of the selection procedure will be short-circuited.

The *application form* is a simple test. How long does it take the woman to complete it? What does she understand or fail to understand about it? How much assistance does she need? What does the information she gives reveal about her? Although most women expect to fill out an application blank, it might be advisable to put them at ease by explaining the general purpose of the form and any parts that might be difficult. This is especially true if it is the first time a woman has completed an employment application form.

Psychological, aptitude, work sample, and other types of *tests* are widely accepted aids in the selection process. However, some women tend to resist being tested. They may not have taken tests since they left school and often feel that they are a little rusty in mathematics or complex business procedures. However, their resistance is not a valid reason for not giving tests; perhaps the tests can be altered. It would be up to the employment interviewer to allay the fears a woman might have about testing.

In order for a test to be legally acceptable, it must be developed by professionally qualified experts. The test must measure the specific qualifications, aptitudes, and skills considered essential for the job. Tests are usually used as only one of many selection tools and should not be considered the sole basis for employment. Care should be exercised to make certain that there is nothing inherent in the test that will discriminate against women. It might even be necessary to establish different standards for women, particularly if mechanical and other typically masculine areas are involved.

Since the interview is the first face-to-face meeting the applicant has with a representative of the company, it is one of the most important phases of the selection process—for both the interviewer and the applicant. One of the interviewer's primary responsibilities is to obtain sufficient information about the applicant so that he can evaluate her qualifications and suitability for the job. He must also supply the applicant with sufficient information about the company, pay, and conditions of employment so that she can determine whether she wants the job. The interview further serves as a supplement to the written application form, tests, references, and other selection tools; and it provides a free and open exchange of information, opinions, and impressions, where interviewer and applicant attempt to determine whether the employment of the latter would be mutually beneficial.

A highly skilled interviewer knows the importance of asking the right questions and avoids asking questions that the applicant can answer with only a "yes" or "no." The interviewer must ask questions that require the applicant to express her opinions, feelings, attitudes, and basic thinking. It is important that the applicant does most of the talking so that the interviewer can gather information and learn about the applicant while she is talking. The interviewer should ask pertinent questions, but shouldn't probe too deeply. All applicants are entitled to the privacy of their personal lives. And the interviewer must remember that women might not be as objective as men concerning their qualifications, their previous work experience, or their attitudes. The truth about many of these things will have to be determined through indirect questioning and by what the woman *does not say* as well as by what she *does say*. The following are examples of questions interviewers should use to draw out the applicant's attitudes and feelings:

How did you come to be interested in this kind of work?
How did your previous supervisors treat you?
What are your hobbies, special interests, and outside activities?
What are your strongest qualities?
What do you least like to do?
What was a typical day like on your last job?
What do your husband and children think about your working?
What do you think are the most important things to keep in mind when trying to get along with people?

Although it may not include every area the interviewer should check, the interview evaluation form, shown in Figure 1, provides a helpful guideline for evaluating applicants. It is particularly valuable when the interviewer has limited interviewing experience or when several applicants are being interviewed for the same position. After the interview is over, if an experienced interviewer thinks that the woman measures up to the requirements of the job and meets the personal qualifications expected, he's probably found the right woman for the job. However, he cannot be certain until reference checks, physical examinations, test results, and all other information are available and evaluated.

The purpose of the *reference check* is to verify and supplement the information supplied by the applicant on the application form and during the interview. Areas to be covered in the check are:

Dates, positions, salaries, reasons for leaving, and eligibility for rehire. (Since it is the policy of some companies not to rehire former employees, the question should be, "If it were not against company policy, would she be eligible for rehire?")
Dependability as evidenced by punctuality, record of absenteeism, completion of work assignments, and overall integrity.
Relationships with co-workers and supervisors.

Work habits based on job performance as compared to other employees in the same type of job.

Ability, motivation, interest, and attitudes toward work.

Experience, if any, in supervising others.

Applicant's strongest and weakest points.

The overall recommendation based on her employment record with
the company.

If the applicant has no previous work experience, her educational
record should be checked. This can usually be done with a telephone
call or letter to the school. The most effective method for checking with
previous employers is to see them in person or to telephone them. A
long-distance call is cheap compared to an employment mistake. (Reference letters carried by applicants have little value. Who has known
an applicant to present one that was not favorable?) Written forms are
often unreliable and inadequate for reference checking. Former employers are reluctant to put unfavorable information in writing because
they cannot be certain of the use that will be made of it.

Figure 1
Interview Evaluation Form

Please complete this form (either during or immediately after the interview)
on applicants being seriously considered for employment.

Applicant's name	Position interviewed for	Date

Directions: Consider each item listed below in relation to the particular job for which you are hiring. Place a check on the line that represents your rating of the applicant.

	Unfavorable	Average	Favorable
1. Appearance — dress and general impression?	___	___	___
2. Age — suitable for the job?	___	___	___
3. Speech — straightforward, pleasing, command of language?	___	___	___
4. Amount of interest in position and company?	___	___	___

	Unfavorable	Average	Favorable
5. Vitality and health—free from chronic or serious illness?			
6. Personality—suitable for job, enthusiastic, friendly?	___	___	___
7. Intelligence—alertness, comprehension?	___	___	___
8. Knowledge—amount known, training needed?	___	___	___
9. Stability—even tempered, able to make job adjustments?	___	___	___
10. Attitude—respectful and cooperative regarding previous employers?	___	___	___
11. Education—appropriate for the job?	___	___	___
12. Experience—appropriate for the job?	___	___	___
13. Family attitudes—does family approve of work? in this company?	___	___	___
14. Family obligations—will care for dependents interfere with performance of the job? lateness? absenteeism?	___	___	___
15. Financial status—salary sufficient to meet obligations?	___	___	___
16. Prior earnings—above or below salary for this job?	___	___	___
17. Transportation—satisfactory and dependable arrangements?	___	___	___
18. Permanence—will applicant remain with company for a reasonable length of time?	___	___	___
19. Working schedule—willing to work the hours required for the job?	___	___	___
20. Previous job relations—why left? ever fired? type of job held?	___	___	___
21. Personal history—why applied here? need to work?	___	___	___
22. Reference checks—type of work history previously established?	___	___	___

EVALUATION:

1. Ideally qualified for job ___.
2. Good prospect ___.
3. Acceptable ___.
4. Fails to meet standards of job ___.

Remarks and additional information:

Interviewer_____

Analyzing and Judging Employment Information

The problems, techniques, and methods involved in hiring women are essentially the same as those for hiring men. In each instance, they should include an appraisal of the job to be filled, the human resources available, and the applicant with the qualifications best suited to the job requirements. The following are among the more significant areas for analyzing and evaluating both interview and employment-related information.

Find out how available she really is for working. Statements such as, "My husband is out of town, and I'm not certain that he wants me to work. But I thought I would get a job and surprise him," or "No, I don't have anyone definitely lined up to care for the children. I thought I would get a job first and then make those arrangements," or "Well, truthfully, I'm not certain whether I'll like working full time, but I thought I'd give it a try," are danger signals for the interviewer. The applicant should resolve these problems before she starts working. Although these are personal problems, it is usually wise to say, "Before we make a final decision concerning the job, we think you should see what arrangements you can make concerning the children," or whatever the problem is. Many women, after being hired, never report for work or work a very short time because they were not really available for work.

Try to determine how long she will work. If a woman is a school teacher, applies for a permanent job at the beginning of the summer, and says that she doesn't really plan to go back to teaching in the fall, caution is the rule. However, if she plans to work only until the hospital expenses are paid, she is a good bet for permanent employment, provided she finds the job satisfactory.

Working may be too much of a hardship on her. She might attempt to work the required schedule; but if it conflicts too severely with the wishes of her husband and with her home responsibilities, she will insist on a change in her schedule or she will stop working altogether.

Don't expect to find men in skirts. Women are women, not men. A woman who gives every indication in appearance, conversation, and manner of being "one of the boys" is seldom as successful as a woman who does not try to be something she is not. Remember that the qualifications of the individual as they relate to the job requirements are the most important consideration. Also, remember that women are often superior to men in many jobs.

Keep economic need and reasons for working in their proper perspective. A woman's economic need is not sufficient motivation to insure her job success. If the salary is lower than her previous earnings, she might remain on the job only until she can find another one at her former salary level or above it. If her reasons for working are to increase the family standard of living or pay for necessities, she should be advised to analyze the net income after taxes. Remind her to include in her analysis a higher tax bracket for two incomes, deductions from her pay for social security and company programs, transportation, child care, parking, purchase of convenience foods, additional clothing, and the possible employment of domestic help. The company might need her services, but neither she nor the company benefits if she discovers with her first pay check that she just can't afford to work.

Don't attach too much or too little significance to women with personal problems. Widows, divorcées, and women who have led difficult lives frequently have indomitable drives that make them excellent employees. The key is to determine how much these factors might interfere with job performance and continued employment. If a woman's husband has just died or if she has just gone through a divorce, it is usually assumed — wrongly or rightly — that the woman's future stability and availability for work is uncertain.

Give proper consideration to age. The most temporary employee is the young girl looking for a husband. The most stable employee is the woman over 35, either married or single, who is career-oriented. Modern women often marry immediately after completing high school or college, have fewer children, and usually do not have any more children after age 27. This means that the youngest child is ready for school when the mother is only 33. According to statistics she still has 32 years of potential employment before retirement. In comparison to younger women, a woman over 35 is more mature and poised, has more self-confidence, requires less supervision, is less likely to change jobs, is more dependable, is absent less often, has learned to dress and converse intelligently, has fewer family problems, is more easily trainable, and will usually be more satisfied with her job. Her superiority in these areas often extends to men as well as younger women.

Evaluate the appropriateness of her educational qualifications. A woman may be underqualified as well as overqualified for certain jobs. If her qualifications are too low, she might experience difficulty in building self-confidence. If she is overqualified, she will be bored. However, she must have the educational qualifications the job requires. It should be a strong point in her favor that she has gone to night school or has taken correspondence courses. However, if she has not completed any of these programs, then it is possible that there was family interference or that she lacked either purpose or ability.

Check health factors thoroughly. Many companies require a physical examination prior to employment. If the job involves continuous standing or physical activity, have a doctor carefully check her back, feet, legs, and her overall ability to meet the physical demands of the job. If she says that, "I've been so nervous the doctor advised me to try working," it is doubtful that the job will be less demanding than the conditions that made her nervous. Make reasonably certain that she will not require too much special attention for physical or emotional reasons.

Get to know her as a person. Inquire about her interests, aspirations, and reasons for wanting to work. If she says she wants to get away from being around just women all day, remember that she might have to work around women all day on the job. If she is headed down the career/self-fulfillment road with a full head of steam, be certain that her enthusiasm can be channeled and not cause conflicts with others, be they women or men. If she attaches too much importance to her femininity by making statements like, "Men have always found me attractive," and "Women are hard to get along with, but I've never had any trouble getting along with men," or if she seems unable to make decisions for herself, remember that the company is looking for women with ability, not prima donnas.

Find out how well she gets along with other people. On the basis of her experiences in school and on other jobs, determine how effective she is in interacting with other people. Her attitude toward others and any offices or leadership positions she may have held are indications of how she is regarded by others. Her hobbies, leisure-time activities, and special interests also reveal whether she prefers people to things.

Determine her motivation and ambition level. Although she may not be aggressive enough or motivated enough to be national sales manager or president, she should be sufficiently motivated to work for job improvement, increased compensation, and promotions. Her expressed and demonstrated goals, desires, and commitments should match those required of the job.

Evaluate all available information concerning her experience with previous employers. Although it is possible for someone to turn over a new leaf, don't count on it. The only safe way to predict future job performance is to make projections based on past performance. What was her experience with previous employers? Did she make satisfactory job adjustments and progress? How well did she get along with her co-workers and supervisors? What was her overall work record? What experience did she gain that might be beneficial on the job for which she is being considered? How long did she stay at previous jobs?

Is the job for which she is being considered in line with her previous job interests? Carefully investigate her reasons for leaving previous jobs. Was she forced to leave or did she want to leave? Why did she want to leave? Generally, a woman with some work experience is a better risk than one who has not worked at all.

Before the company decides to hire the applicant and before the applicant decides to accept the job, a clear understanding of all pertinent issues should be reached. This can best be accomplished by reviewing the following areas:

Time and place to report for work.

Dress regulations or other personal requirements.

Salary, work schedule, position, the kind of work to be done, and other conditions of employment.

The necessity of supplying social security number and other information relative to the completion of all records.

Printed material about the company or the job (if any) that the applicant should read before she starts work.

Parking and food facilities, lockers, medical services, and anything else the company will provide.

Punctuality, attendance, job performance, job adjustment, and whatever else the company expects of its employees.

What the employee can expect from the company in areas of direct and indirect benefits.

After all these areas have been fully reviewed, the applicant should be given the opportunity to ask any questions she may still have and to resolve all her uncertainties about issues that are still not completely clear to her or about areas that were not covered earlier.

PLACEMENT

The results of one survey indicated that more than 98 percent of personnel executives feel that women were superior to men in certain jobs.[1] Companies and personnel executives have had to reexamine their placement practices regarding women because of state and federal laws, the demonstrated ability of women, and favorable experiences of placing women in jobs previously restricted to men.

In an attempt to determine current attitudes and practices, a nation-

---

[1] Edgar S. Ellman, *Managing Women in Business* (Waterford, Conn.: National Foreman's Institute, 1967), p. 108.

wide survey of male and female executives was conducted (by the author). The results include as many replies from women as from men. The question was asked, "What effect should the following assumptions have on management decisions regarding the employment, placement, compensation, and promotion of women?"

It is evident, based on the information in the accompanying table, that opinions vary widely regarding the employment and placement of women and the amount of influence certain factors exert. Both sexes placed more significance on some of these factors than the law permits, thus indicating that a strong informal consideration is exercised in the placement of women. However, the following three areas are now receiving greater attention:

Statistically, women aged 35 and over are likely to remain on a job longer and contribute more years of service than younger women or men. Hence, many women in this category are being placed in junior executive and management training programs and other programs that require long periods of training.

Women have proved that they can function effectively in jobs involving noise, limited physical exertion, less than ideal working conditions, and some overnight and out-of-town travel.

Women have proved themselves to be flexible, agreeable to change, willing to accept responsibility, and adaptable to most company and job demands.

The willingness of companies and individual executives to reexamine their employment and placement practices has increased opportunities for women in many new areas. It has also made available outstanding employee potential badly needed by the company.

Feedback on Recruitment, Employment, and Placement

You can tell that your personnel department is successfully recruiting and hiring qualified women when: positions are promptly filled; the number of women failing to report for work the first day is low; experience proves that applicants understood the conditions under which they were to be employed; an acceptable percentage of women are trainable and make a satisfactory adjustment to the job; the length of time a woman remains on the job and her attendance record are at least average for women in the industry; the minimum number of obviously unqualified or unsuited people are employed.

In the final analysis, if companies expect productive womanpower to be a part of their workforce, they must be willing to make the necessary efforts to accomplish this. Each woman applicant should be viewed

Effect of Assumptions about Women in Business *

Assumptions	No Effect, percent	Significant Effect, percent	Disagree with Statement, percent
Women have a higher turnover rate in the 18–35 age bracket than men in the same age bracket	22	64	14
Women are absent more often than men	29	25	46
Women's medical, insurance, and other employee benefit costs are higher than men's	52	9	39
It's not safe to hire women because of the possible relocation or transfer of their husbands	41	57	2
The number and ages of children can keep women from their work	38	60	2
Both men and women are reluctant to accept supervision from women	52	31	17
The availability of women for travel and work off the premises is restricted	28	60	12
Women usually do not want transfers to other localities	31	61	8
A woman's age can affect her job performance	73	19	8
A husband working in the same company can be a problem	42	53	5
A married woman's job performance is different from a single woman's	75	20	5
Being a widow or divorcée can affect a woman's job performance	88	10	2
The position of a woman's husband affects her job	70	25	5

* See Appendix A for complete results of survey.

as a potential investment from which both the woman and the company will benefit. Wrong decisions result in loss of time and resources to both. The recruitment, employment, and placement processes deserve management's careful, systematic, and thorough attention. Management has the responsibility of providing the financial resources, selection tools, and professionally trained personnel to insure that correct decisions regarding employment and placement of women will be made.

5

Induction, Training, and Development

WHAT the new woman employee eventually does — her attitudes and job adjustment — depends largely on what the company does when she reports for work. She arrives eager, uncertain, anxious, but hopeful. Whether she quickly becomes a productive and long-term employee is strongly influenced by the quality of her induction and training.

INDUCTION

The employment interviewer might tell a woman, "Your references were fine. The medical department has given you a clean bill of health. Your test scores were satisfactory. And in our opinion, you meet all the requirements of the job. You can consider yourself employed, and we will look forward to having you report here on Monday morning at 8:30."

These words do not, by some magic, transform a carefree teenager or wife-mother-homemaker of 20 years into a disciplined, competent, contributing employee. As with all people who have never worked before, transformation to this state involves company procedures designed specifically to convert a new employee into a competent contributor to the company. The newly hired woman is not really a part of the company until she has completed numerous forms, been indoctrinated, and begun to engage in productive work.

Understanding the New Woman Employee

It is not unusual for some women to reach the age of 35 or 40 before applying for their first job. A woman who has never been employed may, with her first job, experience a dramatic transition. She will need intensive company and job orientation. And the company and her supervisors must assume a special responsibility to help her.

The induction program must be designed to meet her needs. Much of this hinges on understanding how she views her new surroundings and what she expects from the job and company. The experienced woman changing jobs needs no more orientation than her male counterpart. But the woman who has never worked before should be given special assistance in the following areas:

The restrictions and disciplines of the job might be a new experience. Physical confinement, repetitive work, curtailment of conversation, and association with men for the first time in a work environment might require her to make stringent and irritating readjustments. Since she might lack self-confidence and therefore feel anxious, she will need generous amounts of reassurance and encouragement. The first few days are critical.

Women are often suspicious of other women, and the supervisor should make a special effort to introduce the new employee to her work group as pleasantly and painlessly as possible. Women who are currently on the job are inclined to greet female newcomers with restraint and questioning appraisal. They have probably developed a social clique and feel a sense of security in it. They know what their relationship is with their supervisor, but they don't know what the newcomer might do to upset the existing social order. At the same time, the newcomer has her own doubts about how she will be accepted, whether she will like her co-workers, and whether she will be able to establish her own status in the sociogram.

Initial contacts and first impressions have a strong and lasting importance. Women form opinions and attitudes very quickly. These will be shaped by the first people the new employee meets and by how she is treated. Her first hour, her first day, and her first experiences will be the most crucial. She will emerge from her early experiences with strong opinions and feelings that will stay with her for as long as she works for the company.

The newcomer's favorable feelings toward the company become the foundation on which to make a positive start. She liked the company well enough to apply for and accept the job. It stands to reason that she wants to continue liking the company, to make good, and, in turn, to be regarded favorably by the company. Her desire for success makes her an excellent candidate for orientation and training activities.

The induction should be adjusted, insofar as practical, to the needs of the individual woman. Regardless of her previous experience, some orientation will be necessary; but the amount and the level are influenced by the experience she brings with her.

Induction should be thorough, and the only guarantee of its completeness and its adaptation for women is a written procedure and checklist. This provides both the company and the woman with the assurance that all essential areas will be covered. A formal program makes the whole process easier and more orderly for everyone concerned.

What Induction Should Provide

The overall purpose of the induction procedure is to provide all new women employees with the information and the opportunity they need so that they can adjust to the work and live up to the company's expectations. During induction, the company should at all times try to develop favorable attitudes and to create the kind of motivation the woman will respond to. Although there are many details, the ultimate result will be a well-adjusted, productive employee. To achieve this, the company should redefine the terms of employment, acquaint the woman with the details and requirements of the job and the company, and try to give her confidence in the company and in herself. All this should be accomplished in the shortest possible time and at a minimum cost.

Responsibility for Induction

The primary responsibility for inducting the new woman employee is generally assigned to the personnel department and to the supervisor of the department in which she will work. The personnel department's responsibilities are:

To welcome her into the company.

To complete all paperwork such as forms required by the government, the company, and the employee. The inexperienced woman might not have a social security number; she might need assistance in making decisions on tax information, life insurance beneficiaries, and hospitalization.

To review salary, work schedule, and other conditions of employment.

To distribute handbooks, benefit guides, and similar company information.

To explain pay plans, merit increases, promotion policies, overtime pay, and incentive pay.

To show films, charts, and other informational aids pertaining to
the company or the industry.

To describe company products, special functions, and other activities.

To explain company policy on attendance and absenteeism.

To clarify training practices and opportunities for self-development
and advancement.

To discuss safety and security measures.

To review the company's publications, bulletin boards, and letters.

To explain various employee recreational activities, associations,
and special privileges to which employees are entitled.

To explain company policies concerning maternity leaves and other
information of special interest to women.

To explain company policy regarding contacts with outsiders in
person and by telephone.

To describe employee services provided by the company and where
and how women employees can obtain assistance.

To conduct a tour of the company's facilities, pointing out things
that may be of particular interest to her.

To encourage her to ask questions she might still have.

To introduce her to her supervisor. (This introduction usually occurs during the employment interview.)

The new employee's immediate supervisor continues the induction
and may delegate parts of it to other experienced people in the department. The supervisor's responsibilities are:

To extend a sincere and warm welcome. It is especially important
for the new employee to feel truly welcome and wanted in the
department.

To engage in a get-acquainted talk with the woman. This often involves a review of information covered in the employment interview, but it will enable the supervisor to get to know the woman.

To review conditions of employment such as hours and schedules.

To introduce the newcomer to other workers in the department.

To tour the department and show the new employee the location of
lockers, time clocks, and other facilities she will be using.

To explain any unpleasant aspects (noise, irregular work schedule)
of the job as well as the pleasant features.

To explain the functions of the department — what it does and
where the woman's job fits into the overall process.

To give the woman an opportunity to ask questions and get more complete details in areas where she still has doubt.

To create and communicate the feeling that the supervisor is interested in her as a person and that her success is of great importance to him. He lets her know that he is available to help her in every way possible. It is extremely important that this rapport and understanding be established between the woman and her supervisor, because this empathy can be her bridge to successful adjustment and job performance.

Once the supervisor has completed all these duties, he turns the new employee over to the person who will assist in her training. However, this does not mean that the new employee will no longer get any attention from her supervisor. She might continue to experience moments of doubt and still need her self-confidence bolstered and the security of knowing that the supervisor approves of her progress, so he should check on her frequently to find out how she is getting along and to offer his assistance. This follow-up should be considered an extension of the induction procedure.

A thorough and systematic induction procedure greatly benefits the new employee. It makes her feel that the company regards her presence and job adjustment as important to its own well-being. And thoroughness at this point can avoid later misunderstandings. It also gives the new employee a feeling of security by showing her what the company will do for her, from personal understanding to professional development. The task of making an inexperienced woman a satisfactory and well-adjusted worker is a considerable challenge. All company personnel should be aware of the orientation process and give special assistance to a new woman employee.

TRAINING

Training is the process by which a worker's competence to perform specific jobs is acquired and then improved upon. The training of women differs only slightly from the training of men; and if women are well trained, the results, in some cases, can be better. The same basic overall training plan used for men can be used for women, with some special adjustments tailored to a woman's needs.

Guides and Objectives for Training

Once the company commits itself to employing women, it must continually provide for women's job performance. The purchased time of

women must be converted as quickly and as efficiently as possible
into personal and company benefits, which is the purpose of training.
Whether on a formal basis in a classroom or on a one-to-one basis with
the supervisor, the training *objectives* for women remain essentially the
same as for men. Only the methods, tools, and range of the activity
vary. The training objectives are:

> To make the overall operation more profitable by reducing the
> amount of equipment, material, and time employees require to
> produce or sell a product or service.
> To provide a fair return for effort expended; this includes pay, rec-
> ognition, job security, opportunity for promotion, and other re-
> wards for a satisfactory job performance.
> To keep up morale and achieve a satisfactory work climate and
> relationship with supervisors.
> To enable new employees to meet the minimum requirements of
> the job and to train more experienced personnel to produce more,
> accept transfers, operate new machines, adapt to new methods,
> increase efficiency, and adjust to changing needs.
> To reduce accidents, waste, and negative factors associated with
> unsatisfactory job activity.
> To increase the woman's willingness to work, her loyalty, her in-
> terest in the job, and her desire to excel.

The company is responsible for designing and making available the
most appropriate training program to meet the special training requirements of women. Most general training can be done on a group basis,
but women also have a need to be trained and coached on an individual
basis. This leaves the primary responsibility for training up to the
woman's supervisor, as it should be, since she will look to her supervisor for instructions, job assignments, reviews of performance, and
other measurements of how she is doing. The supervisor represents the
company to the woman, and her future with the company is largely in
his hands.

The Training Plan

A comprehensive, continuing training plan should be designed and
put in writing. It should cover the training requirements of everyone in
the group, and should include these areas:

> Kinds of training needed by the group as a whole and by each
> woman as an individual.

Most effective methods, techniques, and tools for presenting the training.
Most appropriate time and place for conducting the training.
Preparation of outlines, materials, and visual aids to be used.
Actual implementation of the training plan.

These items can be broadly applied to any training plan for both men and women. It is of particular importance here to keep in mind any special areas that might require extra attention in training women. For example, most women need special training in mechanical operations, business organization, and objective business disciplines. If a woman is inexperienced, she should receive detailed training, repetition of specific points, and thorough explanations of the interrelationships of the various departmental processes and operations. In the training process, it must be made clear to all new employees that they have to accept full responsibility for all the duties of their job, even though some seem unappealing.

A special effort should be made to relate the training to a woman's unique interests and to areas of the job in which she can capitalize on her natural abilities and skills. Her supervisor should remember to praise her when she performs well and to give her ample recognition, encouragement, approval, and assurance of her satisfactory progress. She should receive periodic feedback and progress evaluations so that she can see where she stands in relation to her overall job competence.

When training a woman, a supervisor should always start with what he assumes she already knows and then move to what she doesn't know; present the simple first and then move up to the complicated; keep all explanations to the point; give a reason for each step or phase of training; personally demonstrate what the learner will be required to do and then give the learner a chance to demonstrate and ask questions; check to see how well the learner understands, retains, and applies what she is being taught; use concrete, easy-to-understand illustrations; and set the proper personal example. There is usually a need to relieve tension with humor, examples of past experiences, and case histories to which the learner can relate. Often these are more effective than abstract rules or theories.

Proper training is the basis for production, job satisfaction, and low turnover rates. Usually, the woman who is an outstanding performer in her job is happy with all other aspects of her work environment. If she is a top performer, she seldom becomes dissatisfied to the point of leaving.

The enlightened supervisor knows that training is a continuous process and that all personal contact with his women employees is a form of training. The best method is on-the-job training combined with the supervisor's close, day-by-day follow-up and correction. Before positive results can be achieved, the supervisor must understand that he is dealing with a complete and complex human being, so training must go beyond just learning a skill. He should be able to communicate ideas, attitudes, loyalty, motivation, and interest.

Women are generally responsive to a personalized approach. If inexperienced, they require somewhat greater patience, tolerance, and thoroughness from their supervisor. However, if training is properly structured and conducted, women are excellent learners; and they learn very quickly if the climate and training techniques are structured to suit their special needs and interests. Much of the success depends on the supervisor's own methods and personality.

CONTINUING DEVELOPMENT

Both employee and company can reap tremendous benefits from a woman's willingness to continue her on-the-job development. Development takes two forms: performance improvement in the present position and preparation for promotion by accepting additional duties and responsibilities. Meaningful development doesn't just happen. It is usually the result of careful thought and planning.

The only justification for a development program is the fulfillment of present and anticipated needs of the company. What openings will exist? What skills will be required? When will new positions be available? Answers to these questions depend on how fast the company expects to grow, what products are planned and the skills needed for their manufacture, any positions that might be eliminated because of changes in company structure, and anticipated upward movement and turnover.

The Development Program

What does the company development plan consist of, and to what extent will women participate in it? These questions can best be answered by the following procedures:

An inventory of present female resources. Determine what female resources, skills, and abilities are currently available within the company. If this information is not current, the company should conduct an employee survey to learn which skills and abilities are not being used.

A company-initiated program for, or to include, women. This should be designed to insure that the company is using its human resources to their fullest. If such a program does not exist, women should request one and cooperate with management in implementing it.

Outside educational programs for women. Certain kinds of educational programs are available through colleges and other public agencies. Often the company encourages its employees to attend classes and might agree to pay all or part of the tuition. An ambitious woman will take full advantage of such meaningful training programs, especially those sponsored by the company.

Special assignments and responsibility for women. The company's overall development program might include job rotation, assignment to committees or special projects, delegation of additional responsibilities, job enlargement, and a variety of other methods for developing the general and specific potential of women.

Identifying and promoting top-performing women. The final and most essential test of the whole development program is the company's willingness and success in promoting women on a merit basis. To do this, the company must be able to identify, appraise, and recognize outstanding performers and then be willing to promote them—without regard to sex.

Regardless of the specific system, tool, or method used by the company, the important factor is that an overall plan—one that moves women forward—be in existence.

Responsibility for Her Own Development

An employee is fortunate when she is with a company that has the kind of development program described in this chapter. However, such a program could become a disadvantage if the employee assumes that, because of the elaborate nature of the company's development program, she is relieved of responsibility for her own development. She should remember that every woman will have the same basic opportunity to participate in company-sponsored programs as she and that a woman who wants to advance quickly uses the company program only as a launching pad. She then engages in additional programs on her own initiative, recognizing that her development is her personal responsibility.

6

Maximizing
Results Through
Appropriate Supervision

WHY are women easier to supervise than men? Because women are more visible. They are more vocal in making their preferences and wishes known. They are not submerged icebergs with seven-eighths hidden. Their emotions, their quick and definite reactions, their expressed feelings, and their stated desires regarding the work environment all reveal their basic needs and responses.

Analogously, the customer easiest to convince and sell is the one who makes her feelings, preferences, and objections known. Expressed objections to price provide an opportunity for the salesman to reply, "Yes, but . . ." and proceed to justify the price. But if the customer does not reveal her thinking and remains uncommitted, the salesman is denied the clues he needs. Women workers provide their supervisors with these clues by making their preferences and objections known.

Many men are often more difficult to supervise because they are less responsive, reveal less of themselves, and do not exhibit as much intensity of feeling. But women often communicate their feelings, thoughts, desires, and responses with dramatic clarity, ranging from tears to smiles. As one woman executive stated, "I think men and women might have the same feelings and reactions, but they express them differ-

60

ently." Since women are more sensitive, they tend to be more open in expressing their pleasure or displeasure.

Once a supervisor understands this, he will find his job much easier. Why, then, is there such a continuing problem? Anxiety persists among supervisors because they ignore all the prominently displayed signs. They refuse to read and respond to the clues. The difficulty in supervising women is caused not by the "mystery" surrounding them so much as by the disregard for obvious indicators.

In supervising women, inadequate response is often given to critical factors known to be the motivators of their performance and job satisfaction. Too often, this results from a failure to teach the job thoroughly, to provide clear and complete instructions, to take the time to give individual attention, and to offer recognition and praise. Why? Probably negligence, preoccupation with other things, and failure to consider the ingredients necessary to energize the potential of women.

This chapter seeks to identify and clarify the work-related responses expressed by women. Guides are suggested for achieving both harmony and results. The major areas for implementing supervision — communication, motivation, and so on — will be covered in later chapters.

Establishing Rapport

The supervisor should make a serious effort to establish a relationship of mutual understanding and respect from the first moment he meets the new woman employee. Favorable first impressions lay the foundation for a smooth and comfortable working relationship that is, of course, mutually beneficial. The supervisor who expects permanence and performance should put his best foot forward. He can make a new woman employee feel welcome by letting her know that he is sincerely happy to have her in the department. Women have a great capacity for spotting a phony, so the warmth should be real. He should show an interest in her and make her feel comfortable and secure. He doesn't have to be overly friendly, but he must let her know that a sense of wellbeing exists in the department and that she has an invitation to share in it. The supervisor should also assure her of her probable satisfactory adjustment and future success. And, of course, the supervisor should earn her trust by his manner, actions, and attitude. This will immediately provide her with the ingredients for the rapid development of self-confidence on the job.

A new woman employee should never be confronted with a supervisor whose first words are "Oh, no, not a new employee today. I just don't have time to be bothered. Yes, I did request another person, but I forgot that she would be reporting this morning."

Awareness of Her Needs and Desires

Earlier chapters listed some of the reasons why women work, what they expect in return for their presence and effort on the job, and some of their unique qualities and how these must be handled by management. At this point, the concern is with a woman's expectations regarding the work environment, since it is subject to the supervisor's influence. Her expectations and needs must be met before she will give her best effort to the job.

She has a greater concern for her working environment. A woman might be more concerned than a man with the condition and cleanliness of the rest rooms, the color of the walls and equipment, the amount of noise and dirt, the appearance of the company cafeteria, the friendliness of the people in the department, and the fairness of management. When asked why they choose a certain company, women frequently reply, "Because it seemed like a nice place to work." A clean and comfortable place to work, convenient seating arrangements, equipment specially designed and adjusted to her size and strength, and personal lockers will make her feel the environment is agreeable.

One survey [1] regarding the areas that are important to working women revealed the following information:

Factors Most Desired	*Percentage*
Pleasant work surroundings	79.2
Recognition for work well done	75.4
Fair and equal treatment	68.5
Pleasant people to work with	58.5
Desirable work location	57.7
High wages	46.9
Chance for advancement	34.6

Factors Least Desired	*Percentage*
Overtime	81.5
Educational aid and tuition assistance	79.2
Chance to become a supervisor	61.5
Chance to work closely with bosses	52.3
Time off for personal matters	31.5
Liberal benefits	30.0

[1] Edgar S. Ellman, *Managing Women in Business* (Waterford, Conn.: National Foreman's Institute, 1967), p. 106.

These results indicate that work and human environment are more important to women than advancement or higher wages. Psychologists say that women's nesting instinct is the basis for their desire to dress up work areas with plants, attractive furniture, and colorful typewriters. And women workers are quick to complain about what they consider substandard sanitary conditions.

She has different reactions to safety and dress regulations. Remember that everyone is a distinct individual and has a unique personality and appearance. Rigid dress regulations make a woman one of the herd and deny her the opportunity to express her uniqueness by wearing what she looks best in. Can you expect a woman to accept without complaint standard dress codes after she spends a substantial part of her salary for clothing, hair care, and cosmetics? She wants to look her best, make a good impression on others, and manage her appearance in her own way. If safety clothing is absolutely essential to the job, it should be designed to be comfortable, to minimize hazards around machinery, to provide maximum protection, and at the same time to have as much style appeal as possible. Most women will cooperate when the necessity to wear safety clothing is properly explained to them.

She wants a different kind of supervision. A woman is sometimes more interested in the kind of supervision she receives than in the work she does. She often expects the same sort of relationship with her supervisor that she has experienced with her father and husband. She would like her supervisor to have a thorough understanding of the company and of her job. He should be a careful planner of the department's work activities. He should be neat, clean, and well groomed, and have a pleasant, amiable, and good-natured personality. The supervisor should be able to criticize quietly and constructively, be a good teacher, and recognize and reward good work.

A supervisor should not be too casual and relaxed, too reserved and withdrawn, too aloof, or too strict. When a woman gets the kind of supervision she wants, she responds favorably, and when she doesn't get the supervision she wants, she becomes unhappy and unproductive.

Her moods will come and go. As stated earlier, women are more involved in their home life than men and, therefore, tend to bring their personal problems to work with them. A woman's mood may reflect the state of affairs at home and can be expected to change frequently — even from day to day. Events and interpersonal relationships in the office may also affect her mood. The supervisor shouldn't expect women to be able or willing always to explain their moods. Of course, many women are self-disciplined and very stable and would not exhibit such variations in mood.

She needs a climate of positive firmness and fairness. Being fair is not enough; being firm can elicit negative reactions. But firmness and fairness are necessary ingredients of a smoothly operating work environment. The supervisor must not merely be firm but must state and demonstrate the reasons for his position so that women will find his decisions acceptable and believable.

Supervisors should be careful about granting special favors. Some women feel that if they exert a special effort, they are entitled to request and receive special favors. But the rules that exist apply to everyone equally, and if one woman is granted favors, her co-workers may want and expect the same special treatment.

It is worth noting that women are used to competing with women rather than with men and are, therefore, more concerned with the treatment other women get. Jealousy and strong feelings that they are being treated unjustly may develop if women see another woman receiving special consideration from their supervisor. These feelings are less likely to occur if a man in the department is given special treatment. In short, the fairness a woman expects and the firmness she will accept must visibly apply to all other women employees. The most effective approach to firmness is a clear explanation of what the rules are and the extent to which they will be enforced. When a woman understands the limits of the rules, she cannot be too surprised if her request for a special favor is turned down.

When they encounter this quality and consistency of firmness and fairness, women will feel the security that is so essential to their peace of mind and well-being. The supervisor who does not communicate clearly inevitably finds problems piling up and loses optimum performance and production.

Common Sense in Supervising Women

If the successful supervision of women had to be reduced to one rule, it would be: Supervise women in exactly the same way as men — except more so. It is more important to be thorough in training and communicating with women, to be fair and consistent, to criticize sparingly and praise generously, and to observe all the psychological guides for effective supervisor-subordinate relations.

A man supervising men can be careless in observing some of the guides and still survive without jeopardizing the effectiveness of the workforce. But he had better not practice a hit-or-miss type of supervision where women are concerned. The only safe course, for men and women supervisors, is to know the rules of the company and the fundamentals of good supervision and follow them carefully. Most of these have already been fully discussed earlier in the book and are briefly listed here.

> Openly demonstrate your confidence in her, respect for her, and willingness to cooperate with her.
> Give her individual attention.
> Be courteous and considerate.
> Give her the recognition, appreciation, and praise she needs.
> Be willing to listen and learn.
> Be predictable.
> Clarify and enforce policies consistently.

In addition, the supervisor should be willing to listen to a woman employee's suggestions and complaints. What she has to say might be important to her work and to the department. The supervisor who is afflicted by what one consultant calls the most serious occupational disease of a poor executive—the inability to listen—ignores her message at his own peril. He should encourage women to talk and tell him what's on their minds. And he should listen to what they have to say. She might have some excellent ideas for improving the work area and the work processes. The supervisor should also be willing to listen to small complaints, because they can snowball into something larger. A seemingly small problem can become a major irritation to a woman. If it is ignored she might quit.

And like everyone else, women like to win—at bingo, at finding a bargain, or at their jobs. Pay increases, promotions, supervisory approval, winning employee contests, assignment of additional work, and delegation of responsibility are all evidence that a woman is winning in her struggle for recognition and progress. The supervisor can find many ways to show women that they are winning and give them a satisfactory sense of forward movement.

In short, the best insurance the supervisor has that policies will be followed and that problems will be prevented is to clarify them initially and continuously and to exhibit consistency in his working relationship with women.

Some Don'ts in Supervising Women

Just as there are rules to follow in supervising women, there are also areas that should be avoided. The following are a few "don't" guides:

Don't put women on the spot. They don't like to be put on the spot regarding their work or their personal appearance. Avoid calling attention to their age, faults, family problems, or factors that might tend to downgrade them in the eyes of others. They don't like to be kidded about being overweight, having gray hair, having to wear glasses, or about the way they are dressed. They want to avoid any unfavorable attention.

Don't make unkind generalizations about women. Every woman takes general criticism about women personally. Avoid statements such as, "Temperamental as a woman," "Contrary as an old maid," or "Changeable as a woman." General criticism reflects on the individual and leads to negative reactions.

Don't take her for granted. Don't ever assume that a woman knows that her work is appreciated. If she isn't told that she's doing a good job, she might assume that her performance is unsatisfactory. And a woman should be told *frequently* that she is appreciated and that her position is secure.

Areas for Close Attention

Certain areas in the relationship of the supervisor to the woman employee deserve special attention and handling.

Uniform guides, but individual application. Company rules are made for everyone, but they must be applied individually. Women need to understand the importance of policies, the reasons for their existence, and why they should be followed. But at the same time, rules should be applied to fit the individual and each situation.

Rigidity versus flexibility. How rigid should safety rules and job performance standards be? Too much rigidity places women in irritating and stifling straitjackets. Too much flexibility leads to a breakdown of discipline and job achievement. Perhaps the only reasonable guide is the one given by the basketball coach to a freshman trying to make the team: "You have to develop the right touch. If you shoot it too hard or too soft, you'll miss the basket. You have to think about it and work at it until you have the right feel for dropping the ball through the hoop."

Developing a comfortable climate. Climate determines the morale of employees. The supervisor has the opportunity to initiate and maintain the kind of climate in which women will want to give their best effort. A good climate results when there is effective communication, understanding, counseling, training, respect, and all other factors that affect the feelings of women employees.

Deciding when supervisory intervention is necessary. The supervisor must maintain harmony and must know when to take charge of problem situations, or the following situation never would have developed: For almost a year, at least 25 percent of the women in the department were not getting along. The situation would never have gotten out of hand if there had been strong supervision. If the first petty incident had been discussed and settled, the problem would have ended, and everyone would have gone back to work. But when asked to intercede, the personnel manager said, "Don't bother me with such petty stuff; let them settle it among themselves." If they had been able to settle it themselves, he wouldn't have been approached in the first place. And so the fighting continued, creating rifts and bitterness between women who needed to work closely with each other.

Avoid involvement in personal affairs. The supervisor should avoid becoming involved in the personal affairs of his employees. It is not the supervisor's role to judge what her husband and children do or how she solves her personal problems. He should be extremely cautious in giving advice or stating his opinions.

In sum, if women are to be supervised successfully, supervisors must recognize that women's conditioning from birth has made them different from men. However, their differences do not reduce their value as employees.

Supervisors of large numbers of women have found that the same common-sense rules and practices that prove successful in supervising men prove equally effective in supervising women. The jobs women are expected to do might be complicated, but it's a good bet that these jobs will be no more complicated than women's home responsibilities.

Don't underestimate the great potential of women—their talent, their intelligence, their physical capacity, and their overall ability to make a profitable contribution to the success of the department and company. The potential is there. What it ultimately amounts to depends largely on the company's success in creating the kind of human and leadership environment that women can respond to.

7

Influence of
Management Innovations
in Supervising Women

WHEN the company is concerned with women as employees and customers, special attention must be given to the philosophy, practices, and style of management that affect women. Certain styles have proved to be more effective than others. And since management style in relation to women is of significant economic importance to the operation of the business, the most effective styles of management should be practiced.

One day a woman who had been a cashier in a credit office for ten years came into the personnel office and asked to see the personnel director. She told this story:

"I'm resigning. I'll give two weeks' notice if you want me to, but I've got to get away from that man."

"What's the problem?" asked the personnel director.

She replied, "Look, I've told you this before. Mr. Waters is impossible to work for, and I don't mind telling you that several other girls in the department are also planning to leave. You just can't please that man. He thinks he's the only one who knows how to do anything. And he doesn't have the common courtesy to listen to anyone else or to consider anyone else's ideas. I could mention dozens of times that

I've told him something wouldn't work, but he stubbornly insisted that it be done his way. Then he bawled me out because it didn't work out right. There are so many ways we would like to help him, but he doesn't want any help. Well, maybe someday he'll learn that he can't do everything himself. I'm really sorry to be leaving. Actually, I like the company and the other girls, but not enough to put up with what I have to take from that man."

A supervisor like this not only causes turnover to be high, but substantially reduces the performance and potential of the people who remain on the job. Hence we can see that the style of management has a great effect on the achievement of women. They will not accept poor management. They'll resist it, fight to change it, undermine it, kill it with rumors, and if all else fails they'll leave.

Blake and Mouton, in *The Managerial Grid,* graphically identify the extremes of management styles. At one end of the scale is management that gives ". . . thoughtful attention to needs of people for satisfying relationships that lead to a comfortable, friendly organization atmosphere and work tempo." At the other end is management that believes "Efficiency in operations results from arranging conditions of work in such a way that human elements interfere to a minimum degree." The middle ground is represented by management that believes that "Adequate organization performance is possible through balancing the necessity to get out work while maintaining morale of people at a satisfactory level." [1] The middle position is most acceptable and will produce the best results where women are concerned. Along the scale are many styles that affect the performance of working women:

Task management — produce or perish.
Country club management — win friends and influence people.
Middle of the road management — firm but fair.
Impoverished management — don't rock the boat; do as little as possible.
Team management — people support what they help create.

The most desirable of these is team management. But this is true only if the team has a recognized and functioning quarterback who is willing to call the signals in the huddle.

Women's View of Management Styles

Styles of supervision in American business have substantially changed over the years. Sweatshop tactics have largely been eradicated,

[1] Robert R. Blake and Jane Srygley Mouton, *The Managerial Grid* (Houston: Gulf Publishing Company, 1964), p. 10.

paternalism is disappearing, and new, professional management styles
have emerged. J. Sterling Livingston of Harvard conducted a year-long
study that sought to determine the most effective style of management.
He interviewed supervisors, their subordinates, and their superiors in
attempting to discover the key to management effectiveness. He was
able to identify three distinctive management styles: (1) directive
management, (2) nondirective management, and (3) interactive management. These three styles are examined in relation to their effectiveness in managing women.

Directive management is practiced by the manager who is self-
confident and likes responsibility. He maintains tight controls over
his employees. He does not seek ideas from others and sets inflexible
standards. This manager believes that the best way to get top performance is through the use of reward and punishment. In short, he
makes it absolutely clear that he is boss and that he makes the decisions.

This type of manager was confronted by a woman in the branch
office of a bank. She reacted to her boss's directive style by saying,
"I'll do the job the best way I can, but he had better leave me alone. If I
didn't have to work, and if this office wasn't convenient for me, I
wouldn't stay here five minutes. That man's a tyrant. I didn't think
there were men left in business like that. I'll do what's necessary to get
by, but he's not going to get anything beyond that out of me. He doesn't
deserve it." This is the typical reaction of women to aggressive, tyran-
nical managers. This style is offensive to them, and they'll fight it in
their own ways. And, if they see they're losing the fight, they'll leave.

Nondirective management is used by the manager who believes
that if good people are at work, they can be left alone to get the job
done on their own. He believes in self-direction and control, and he
knows that people work for recognition and that if they are made to
feel competent, they will do the right thing. He is inclined to manage by
consensus, allowing the work group to make decisions. He provides a
relaxed, flexible environment. He believes that this will make people
happy and cause them to do better work. Unfortunately, this doesn't
always work out. His subordinates are neither happy nor productive,
especially if they are women. Women want definite direction and policies; they want to know what is expected of them. They assume that
final decisions will be made by the boss and are disappointed and
frustrated if he abdicates his responsibilities.

The assistant manager of an insurance office resigned, giving this
reason: "I know that Mr. Knox wants to be easy with us and wants us
to like him, but he's the most frustrating boss I've ever worked for. He
simply won't make decisions. He wants to spend all day discussing a
simple problem. When the deadline is on top of us and he *has* to decide,

we're already behind schedule because so much time has been wasted. If he would just spend less time trying to get everyone's opinions and go ahead and make a decision, everyone would be better off. It has frustrated me so much that I don't enjoy the work anymore. I think I'd be happier somewhere else."

Women simply want a reasonably secure and definite climate in which to work. It gives them a sense of direction, makes them feel more comfortable, and creates a more satisfying and productive environment.

Interactive management is practiced by the manager who is flexible, who interacts with his subordinates, involves all members of the team in the department's activities, reviews plans with subordinates, and has a relationship with them that is much like that of a team coach with his players. He values his subordinates' ideas and lets them know it; he makes them feel involved in decision making, especially in those areas that influence their future. Yet everyone knows that he alone makes the final decisions and that he doesn't shirk his responsibilities.

A layout artist was talking with a friend about her job and supervisor. She said, "If all bosses were like mine, no one would have any reason to complain. He asks for my ideas, and I really feel that I'm helping to run the department. Oh, when push comes to shove, he makes the final decision. But, after all, that's his job, and I'm glad he has to do it and not me. I work hard, but I enjoy every minute of it. He's great, and I'd do anything in the world for him."

The directive style produced results for only a short period of time, and morale declined, resentment grew, and subordinates either left or found ways to drag their feet. The nondirective style failed to provide the disciplined environment, expression of desired results, and willingness to assume responsibility for leadership that are necessary for high morale and high production. Therefore, Dr. Livingston concluded from his study that interactive management was the most effective of the three, especially where women are concerned, because the manager who uses it recognizes the individuality of each of his subordinates and adjusts and adapts himself to them. This flexibility combines with understanding, patience, and firmness to create a climate conducive to top job performance and high morale.

The Influence of Professional Management

Each year approximately 75,000 middle- and top-level managers of both sexes attend American Management Association meetings in New York and throughout the world to learn to be "professional" managers. Professional management is the most significant and the most used style of management in practice today. For our purposes here, it must be viewed in light of its effect on women's job performance and opportunities.

Lawrence A. Appley, while president of AMA, defined professional management as ". . . the guiding of human and physical resources into dynamic organization units which attain their objectives to the satisfaction of those served and with a high degree of morale and sense of attainment on the part of those rendering the service." This kind of management is considered *professional* because, as with other professions, it has a body of knowledge, follows a scientific approach, involves specific skills and tools, adheres to a code of ethics, has a required discipline, and its skills and techniques are transferable from one environment to another. Its framework is the setting of goals and objectives, the organization of human and other resources, the establishment of standards of performance and controls, the appraisal of results in relation to expectations, and the response and correction for future improvement. Professional management provides the opportunity for making progress along the way and insures objective evaluation of results.

Perhaps the most significant characteristic of professional management is that it quantifies the various aspects of management and the work process. Rather than dealing in generalities — which can rarely be understood and can cause confusion — it is oriented toward specifics, such as numbers, percentages, time, dollars, and other bench marks of performance, which can be defined, communicated, and agreed upon. It provides orderliness, results-oriented activity, maximum human involvement, and both tangible and intangible rewards.

But how does this evolution in management styles and techniques affect the employment and opportunities of women? For one thing, it significantly enhances their opportunities in all areas. It is the kind of management that is concerned with quantitative factors, not sex or personalities. It provides no basis for discrimination, but rewards in accordance with performance.

Professional management provides the greatest boost imaginable to the opportunities for women to achieve and benefit in proportion to their contribution. They want a chance to prove themselves, to be evaluated as individuals, and to receive the respect and status of rank. Professional management gives them this opportunity. But at the same time, it requires acceptance of responsibility and accountability for getting the work done and achieving the desired results. It gives women the opportunities they have been seeking, but it will also gauge accurately whether they measure up. The chief advantage professional management offers to women is its objectivity in assessing performance.

The Influence of EDP

The revolution in business created by electronic data processing gives an added boost to the opportunities for women. EDP handles, electronically and at fantastically high speeds, data recording, processing, and analysis that were previously manual operations when they were done at all. For example, a state bank estimated that by the year 2000, if EDP were not available, every person living in the state would be required to work for the bank in order to handle all their paperwork.

Perhaps the prime advantage of EDP is that it frees women from much of the routine, low-level clerical work to which they have been traditionally relegated. They can now program and operate computers and in general perform higher-level, more creative, interesting, and challenging jobs. But more importantly, women, now free from low-level work, are available to move up in the ranks of management.

This objective approach to management and decision making leads to promotions on merit rather than on subjective opinion. Women will be evaluated on the basis of statistical results. Thus, they will have the opportunity to prove that they can get the job done and thereby receive their just rewards.

In sum, it is management's continuing responsibility to create and implement the kind of leadership most advantageous to the achievement of company goals. And since the best interests of the company are served when women are employed, the company should be prepared to practice the management styles that have been proved to work best with women.

In mastering and implementing the specific leadership techniques covered in Part III, the reader should give careful attention to developing and using the most effective management styles and processes. The success of this effort will substantially influence the degree of success that individual supervisors can expect in their working relationships with women.

part three

Mastering Specific Leadership Techniques for Managing Women

8

Achieving
Effective Communication
with Women

BEFORE women can move from raw potential to actual achievement, they must pass through channels of training, motivation, and response, The link and energizer for these is the communication loop from supervisor to employee and back to supervisor.

Every position in the company, from president to first-line supervisor to subordinate, is a crucial link in the information chain. As messages reach each level they are subject to blockage, filtering, and distortion and then they continue on their way. Communication that travels from one layer of authority to the next is analogous to an electrical current passing through a transformer. It can be stepped up, stepped down, or changed in form. But in each case, the transformer determines what will be transmitted.

Bridge to Job-Related Understanding

A woman will give her best effort to her work only if she understands what she has to do, why she is expected to do it, and to what extent she is achieving the goals. If she comes to the job with limited or no experience, her supervisor is confronted with a formidable task in communication. The supervisor ultimately spends about 90 percent of his time communicating with her in some manner. Although corporations develop highly sophisticated techniques and systems for communication, by far the most effective method is still the one-to-one, supervisor-subordinate interaction.

The supervisor must recognize and respond appropriately to the fact that communication provides the bridge over which women must travel to reach their personal job goals. Job security, supervisory approval, job satisfaction, job performance, as well as the more personal aspects of the job all depend on his ability to communicate and her willingness to accept what he has to say. Women value the supervisor's efforts to communicate, but they place great importance on what he fails to say — his unintentional messages. He must learn how to foster an atmosphere in which women will accept his supervision, ideas, and changes.

Communication as an Influence and Control

Communication is the process through which the company influences and controls job behavior. This is not a manipulative influence or a negative, restrictive control, although it could possibly degenerate to these levels. Influencing and controlling the performance of employees is the supervisor's job. His success in managing the department and her success on the job depend on how well he is able to discharge this responsibility. Both what and how he communicates are important. He should be clear and firm, and he should believe in what he says, for only then will his subordinates trust him.

Effective communication opens the door to positive, purposeful job activity. It is assumed that each supervisor knows what is to be achieved and how these goals can be reached. He must then communicate to his staff what they must do to fulfill their roles and his expectations. He should also make clear the *purpose* of a specific job activity.

Influence and control provide the framework for job behavior. They must include the words, symbols, promises, know-how, specific information, and motivation that will cause the desired activity to occur. And controls provide accurate measurement of what is occurring and what action needs to be taken to improve the quality of the work.

What the Company Expects and What Women Expect

The ultimate purpose of communication should be to fulfill the expectations of both the company and the woman involved. This includes a particularly heavy dose of what the company expects of her during working hours. But the company's efforts are wasted if it does not take into consideration the wide range of expectations a woman brings with her to the job. Let's consider what both expect:

What the Company Expects from the Woman	What the Woman Expects from the Company
Regular and prompt attendance.	Job security.
Her best efforts.	Advancement and compensation in direct proportion to her contribution.
Harmonious relationships with her supervisor, her associates, and the public.	Pleasant and safe working conditions.
Constructive suggestions.	Cooperative associates.
Reasonable response to training and supervision.	Reasonable employee benefits and provision for her job-related needs.
Acceptance of the company's purpose — whatever it may be.	Competent, understanding leadership.

If the company ignores her needs or if she ignores those of the company, nothing will be accomplished. It is possible that words and sounds will be transmitted, but understanding and responsive action will not result.

Barriers to Communication

Getting someone to understand what you understand is a difficult job, even when conditions are ideal. But when male supervisors have to transmit complex mechanical or business information to their female subordinates, the difficulty is multiplied, especially if the latter are inexperienced in business. There's no doubt that women are better informed than men on a great many subjects, but these subjects are not necessarily job related. Those subjects and related terminology that have become second nature to the supervisor might have a strange sound to women. It is often advisable to supply women with a list of the words peculiar to the business or to her job.

Perhaps a look at some of the barriers and difficulties involved in communicating with women will encourage the supervisor to give the subject special attention. (These are not unique to women; men, too, face the same problems.)

Each woman is inclined to create a kind of mental deafness to something she does not want to hear. It may be an idea she does not want to accept, information from people she doesn't like, or messages that are difficult to understand and respond to. In some cases, she might have stereotyped ideas that influence what she accepts and believes. What she believes is significantly influenced by her attitudes toward the communicator and the information involved.

She often rejects messages when she is suspicious of the motives of the communicator.

She has a tendency to ignore information which she feels she knows or to which she is already opposed.

Her current emotional state or mood will influence her acceptance of and responses to information.

She is inclined to interpret information in terms that fulfill her desires and expectations.

She evaluates information according to her own set of values.

The difference in rank between her and the communicator might inhibit her understanding and acceptance.

The wise manager must remember these barriers as he attempts to communicate with women. His awareness will provide him with guides for planning and executing all communications with women—from highly complex written information to simple, spoken person-to-person contact. It often helps to personalize communications and to include a touch of humor.

If supervisor and subordinate are poles apart, expectations, symbolic understanding, and word usage will fall on barren ground. A rapport must be created that promotes mutual confidence and acceptance of what both people are attempting to communicate. The atmosphere of the moment is the byproduct of the experiences each person has had with the other. The basis on which women will be open to communication is this accumulation of trust, respect, fairness, kept promises, and the overall climate that has been created.

Key Factors in Communicating with Women

There are three vital factors that can insure effective communication with women. The first is that the supervisor must make certain he is getting through to the subordinate. Does she really understand what he is saying? Does she have the same mental picture of the problem, the activity, and the course of action as the supervisor? Communication must continue until a thorough understanding has been reached.

The second factor is the formation of a strong conviction that what she has been told is true and that it serves her best interests. Once understanding and conviction have been reached, the third factor, responsive action, naturally follows. Responsive action is the whole purpose of communication, whether the action is increased loyalty and effort, greater productivity, better customer service, increased job competence, or general overall improvement. When the desired responsive action is not forthcoming, communication has failed.

The techniques and methods used to communicate with women might include person-to-person conversation, employee handbooks, contests, bulletin boards, information and reading racks, meetings, company magazines and newspapers, letters, pamphlets, movies, film strips, visual aids, posters, company reports, telephones, suggestion systems, and an almost endless variety of other media. However, the most effective method is still the day-to-day working relationship between supervisor and employee. A personnel executive defined communication as "Not a process, but a relationship." This is especially true where women are involved. Regardless of the method used, communication should involve the following facets if it is to work effectively with women:

Feedback is necessary in order to test understanding.

Several different methods should be tried since some will prove more effective than others. (Face-to-face communication is often the most complete and effective method.)

The communicator should be sensitive to the receiver, whose moods and receptivity greatly influence the result.

The communicator should be aware of how each message is interpreted.

If possible, allow sufficient time for the gradual acceptance of new ideas or changes.

Language should be chosen with care so that understanding is assured and opportunities for misunderstandings are eliminated.

Repetition is usually necessary—once is not enough.

Furthermore, communication styles and techniques, like food and clothing, vary in acceptance and appeal—it all depends on the individual receiver. The specific methods selected for communicating with women should be the ones most likely to achieve the desired response. Experience has proved that the most successful approaches are feminine in orientation, in that they make extensive use of terms and symbols that appeal to women and are presented on the basis of her self-interest. Contests and competition are also effective.

Too much communication is wasted. It elicits no response. A department store executive once remarked, "At least half of our advertising dollar is wasted, but we don't know which half!" The same can be said about attempts to communicate with women, but since we don't always know what will be wasted and what will work, we continue our attempts. The supervisor should limit communications with women in groups but should deal with each employee on an individual basis. Eventual success hinges on the degree to which the message is clear.

Clarity and exactness are influenced by the language used, the amount of planning involved, the follow-through, and the willingness of management to engage in communication as carefully as it approaches production and sales. Communicating with women consists of certain ingredients and techniques that must fit together in the proper mix before desired results can be expected.

Guides for Eliciting Desired Response

Try to put yourself, the communicator, in the place of your woman subordinate, the receiver. How would you receive the message? How well would you understand what you are supposed to do? Would you understand how the job is to be done? Is everything crystal clear? Are there any questions left unanswered such as how well? how much? at what time? and in what manner? What is the specific action expected to be? Understanding these factors will determine the action your subordinate is willing to take.

The following checklist should prove beneficial in attempting to elicit results through communicating with women:

Clarify in your own mind ideas, information, policies, changes, and requests for action before attempting to communicate them.

Put them in writing. Test them and then make any necessary revisions.

Be sure of the purpose of the communication. What is it to accomplish? Adapt communication to accomplish the desired goals.

Be sure that the total physical and human environment is appropriate for communicating. Obviously the climate on the production line or in front of a file cabinet will be different from that of your office.

Remember that regardless of their original purpose and intent, communications may be interpreted differently when received. Try to plan, anticipate, and make adjustments in advance in order to insure that it will be received as intended.

The message will be received well if something helpful or beneficial to the woman is conveyed in it. This opens receiving channels and elicits favorable responses. Solve current problems, but also strive for long-range improvements. If communication is for the purpose of putting out fires, plan preventive measures for the future so that the problem will not recur.

Scrutinize the results of your efforts. This provides the most accurate gauge for future communication.

Be as interested in understanding the woman involved and the difficulties she faces as you are in trying to get her to understand you.

Remember that actions speak louder than words. The most persuasive communication is your personal example and action.

Unintentional Communication

Often the unintentional message is a more effective means of communication than the intentional message. Women are very perceptive. They have an intuitive feel for the thinking and actions of other people. Women have been known to suspect that a problem exists without any overt evidence. When they ask, "What's wrong?" and nothing has been said to lead them to believe that there is anything wrong, their acute perception and sensitivity are at work. Thus, when dealing with women on the job the things you don't say or do are as important as those you do say or do. Female supervisors tend to be more aware of these so-called hidden communicators than male supervisors. Women understand each other, and often many impulses pass through communications channels that men do not notice or intentionally initiate; therefore, men fail to recognize their existence or importance.

When women are involved, the wise supervisor must recognize the unintentional influences. Tone of voice, speed of movement, what is not said, a shrug of the shoulder, a lifted eyebrow, and a hundred other nonverbal indicators provide information to the alert female. She receives and interprets these unintentional communications, and often the messages she registers in this way overshadow the carefully planned program of the company and supervisor.

Supervisors of women, especially men, are never sufficiently aware of the significance of this kind of communication. It is in this area that they encounter the greatest confusion and misunderstanding. Supervisors are constantly heard to ask in bewilderment, "Well, how in the world did she get an idea like that?" Men are constantly amazed at the messages women receive and act on. The failure to communicate overtly doesn't keep certain messages from getting through.

So the supervisor of women should deliberately engage in as much of the right kinds of overt communication as possible. If he does not plan and exercise some direction and control, chaos can result. Even after he has given careful, systematic, and continuous attention to planning and implementing the right kinds of communications, there will still be a significant amount of unintentional and uncontrolled communication going on. He has to do everything possible to maintain a constant, positive thrust and supply the right information in order to partially counteract what he has less control over.

Priming the Communication Pipeline

The flow of information through the communication pipelines needs boosters. Ways should be developed to cause greater flow from management downward to women and from women upward to management. The techniques of working with individuals and groups, a willingness to listen, suggestion systems, and the like will promote this two-way flow.

Encouraging the flow downward to women. Once management has established goals and purposes, women should be informed of what they are. Plans, policies, changes, methods, employee benefits, work schedules, and a wide-ranging variety of other information must flow down through the various levels of management to reach every subordinate level. Special care should be exercised to insure only minimum amounts of filtering, alterations, and spillage as the information flows downhill. Downward communication should involve a deliberate, planned, systematic, and continuing program that will bring about the desired response from the individual and group.

Overcoming gravitational forces to increase the upward flow. Management is not smart enough to know all the answers: the thoughts and feelings of women, their changing aspirations, the kinds of communications to which they will respond, and the specific things they want to know. So management should get women involved in the communications process as communicators and as receivers. The upward flow can be significantly stimulated by demonstrating to women that management is interested in them—that it values their opinions, is willing to listen, and maintains a leadership climate that is conducive to communication. This upward flow, like an artesian well, will occur only if the pressure is uncapped and the impediments to its flow are eliminated. Women want to talk, to express their opinions, and to make their wishes known; but they must be made to feel that their supervisors are interested.

Using boosters. Many organizations make effective use of groups and systems to boost the two-way flow of information. These include suggestion systems that encourage each woman to pass along information—special committees, employee contests and various promotions, group meetings, educational programs, and a variety of others. The ultimate purpose of these programs is to cause the information to flow, thereby leading to appropriate action on the part of each woman involved.

Effective Communication with Women

Every supervisor working with women is constantly faced with the responsibility of supplying the vital ingredients of trust, understanding, conviction, and response to his employees. In order to do this, he must develop a master communications plan—one that is constantly being changed and updated; communicate the right information, in the right amounts, at the right times; be willing to consult with others, seek advice, accept feedback, and listen; make communications colorful, interesting, clear, understandable, and acceptable to women; win the attention and interest of women before attempting to communicate with them; execute the program thoroughly, because the plan has little value unless it is properly implemented; and follow through with overt and purposeful action, since communication will fall on deaf ears unless it is backed with action.

It is essential to keep all employees informed—and women are no exception. As a matter of fact, they will insist on it. Management's failure to inform them results in misinformation gained through the various grapevines and other available sources. Women will not work efficiently, feel secure, attain a sense of well-being, reach a point of acceptable job satisfaction, and will probably not remain on the job unless they know what is going on around them. They want to know what is happening in the company, especially those things that might affect them and their jobs.

If a favorable climate exists and every reasonable effort is made to keep a woman informed, she will respond with her best effort. Communicating with women requires repetition, constancy, sincerity of purpose, clarity, feelings as well as words, and supportive action. When the right kind of effort is made, they in turn will engage in responsive action appropriate to achieving the goals expected of them.

9

Motivation: Maximizing Women's Contribution

THE critical test regarding the employment of women is the value of the contribution they make to the purposes of the enterprise. The premise of this book is that women have vast potential, and this chapter seeks to provide guides that motivate women to make the most valuable contribution possible.

Potential versus Actual Contribution

Objectively, a woman's compensation, intangible rewards, promotions, and overall opportunities should relate directly to the contribution she makes to the goals of the company. Therefore, women who exert their best efforts and who are effective benefit both themselves and the company. Their response to the company's goal expectations is their means of earning and receiving what they seek and expect from their jobs. The answers to the following questions are basic to the motivation of women:

What are the specific performance goals for this woman in her present job?
What is her current performance level?
What is her maximum potential performance level?
What quantitative achievements should be expected once she has reached her maximum potential?

> What specific changes must occur before the desired performance
> level is reached?
> What overall program must be developed for this woman in order
> to bring about the desired change?
> What specific motivational factors will achieve the response desired
> in her particular case?

The key to the successful motivation of women is to see and understand what their full potential is and then to communicate this knowledge to them so that they understand it, believe it, find it acceptable, and respond to it positively.

If there is a credibility gap between what she believes and what the company and her supervisor tell her, the woman will not respond to motivational efforts. A woman's job effort, loyalty, dependability, and permanence are in direct proportion to what she thinks the company can and will offer her in return for her contribution. And so, analyses of what she really wants from the job, her reasons for working, and the kind of supervision she wants must be made. Otherwise all efforts at motivation will be a waste of time.

Why Attempts to Motivate Misfire

The scattergun approach to motivation will not work. Male-oriented inducements will probably not work either. Women have special interests and needs that must be met. Attempts to motivate them will continue to misfire unless they provide the special kinds of rewards or conditions she wants. Here are some specific reasons why attempts to motivate women are often ineffective:

> Failure to establish and identify specific goals and objectives in
> quantitatively meaningful terms.
> Failure to use motivational approaches that are acceptable and appealing.
> Failure to involve women in establishing their own goals and in
> seeking their own contributions so that goals can be achieved.
> Failure to communicate with women in language they can appreciate.
> Failure to be convincing, to get across what is really expected, and
> to provide specific steps for making the desired response possible.
> Failure to remember that women need repetition, continuous attention, and constant readjustment in line with the changing situation and their interests.

Failure to recognize that the most critical ingredient for motivation is the personal loyalty of the woman. A woman assistant manager once said of her boss, "He has it made. He won the loyalty of the women around him, and from that point on his success was assured."

Women can be motivated; they can be energized to achieve maximum performance, but only through processes tailored to meet their needs and desires. This is the crux of the behavioral scientist's approach: an attempt to stimulate participation and the response of individuals in accordance with their threshold of acceptance.

Basic Motivational Guides

Certain guides are fundamental in the motivation of women. Techniques must be approached with an understanding of the psychological principles involved. The following paragraphs serve as a frame of reference.

The concept of motivation assumes that a *change* is desirable. It might be anything from an increase in sales to getting to work on time.

Motivation results from the efforts, activities, and influence of the supervisor that cause desired changes to occur. These efforts might take the form of training, interviews, coaching, contests, or discipline.

The woman must have a clear understanding of expectations or performance goals. How many dollars in sales are expected? How many units should be produced per hour? What quality of work is expected?

The woman must understand the specific number and kinds of changes that should occur in her performance. This consists, first, of discussion on the gap between present and expected performance. How much improvement is involved?

The woman must understand the adjustments in behavior or performance that she must make so that the desired goal will be reached. What is she expected to do differently? What exactly are those differences?

A program must be developed that will result in the desired changes and the achievement of expected goals. This includes time, methods, remedial programs, and specifics that will provide the stepping stones for change.

The woman must understand why the change is beneficial to her and why it justifies the additional effort required. Questions such as "Why should I make this change?" or "How do I benefit from the change?" should be answered. Either positive or negative responses will prove the desirability of the change to her. She might anticipate an increase in pay or a promotion if she meets the established goals.

The woman's response will be in direct proportion to her ability to make the change and the desirability of the end result of the change.

Each response and result either weakens or strengthens all future motivational efforts. If the supervisor requests change and leads the woman to believe that she will benefit from it, the degree to which she really does benefit will either reinforce or jeopardize all subsequent motivational efforts.

The quality of the relationship between the motivator and motivated, the amount of mutual confidence and respect, the credibility of all communications, and the sum total of all past experiences provide the proper motivational climate for change.

Motivation is possible when the woman wants certain things from the job relationship. She must come to understand that the benefits she hopes for will be attained only through her own efforts. However, on the occasion when her own goals are satisfied but those of the supervisor are not, she must be stimulated to go beyond her present level in order to be considered a satisfactory performer by the company.

In motivating women, it should be remembered that hard, accurate, objective facts will not always elicit response. As Peter Drucker pointed out in a series of films produced by the Bureau of National Affairs, the way women feel about facts is often more important in determining response than the facts themselves. Each woman interprets facts and information in terms of her own understanding and often reacts with emotion rather than with logic. Thus, a supervisor who wants to motivate his female subordinates must make certain that emotional factors have been recognized and that related problems have been resolved.

The overall work climate — the supervisor, the work itself, co-workers, and the company — greatly influences motivation. What sort of environment is now being provided for the woman? How does she feel about it and respond to it? The supervisor should seek to construct, change, or improve all human and physical influences to promote the kind of climate most conducive to receiving favorable responses from women.

Keys to Maximum Commitment and Results

"Give her what she wants and she'll be eating out of your hand." Although this is an oversimplification, it does identify the correct approach for eliciting the kind of commitment needed for top job performance. The obvious way to find out what a woman wants is simply to ask her. It is up to the supervisor to find practical ways of giving women what they want. Of course, this has to be done within his operating framework and in accordance with the options and limits available to him.

Pinpointing the wants of women subordinates requires active rather than passive supervision. This does not mean that the supervisor should interfere or constantly look over his subordinates' shoulders, but he should actively provide the things for which women are willing to work. He should never expect to pay women with "just money" and get results. It won't happen. Certainly women expect fair pay and benefits, but money is not enough. The real source of their inner commitment is the intangible, human ingredient. It is in this delicate area that the supervisor finds his greatest opportunity to motivate women.

A woman will respond only minimally until she has a clear concept of the direct relationship of her contribution to the overall result. So long as she fails to see the relationship, she will not go all out to achieve. The company and the supervisor should institute a system that insures this cause-and-effect result.

Raising Women's Expectations

Do women really believe that extra effort will enable them to get what they want from the job? How attractive are the rewards for which they are being asked to work? If they do not find the results appealing enough to justify the effort, or if they doubt their probable success, they will not be willing to risk the extra effort.

An increase in women's expectations depends on providing "cause and effect" conditions based on merit — not sex. The rewards should be made as desirable and attractive as possible by the supervisor and the company. Efforts should be made to boost the expectations of women, to enable them to believe that they can produce, achieve, and be rewarded in accordance with results. The situation as explained to the woman must be believable; it must be realistic; it must appeal to her as an individual; and it must reinforce her ideas of what she wants from the job.

Motivation Through the Work Itself

Hobbies and games lure devotees because they provide the stimulation, the interest, the challenge, the competition, the involvement, the personal contacts, and the satisfactions necessary for motivating someone to do something.

Robert N. Ford conducted a series of unique experiments at the American Telephone and Telegraph Company, and concluded that job enrichment can be a key to motivating women to higher levels of performance. He also discovered that changes, improvements, and enrichment of the contents and activities of the job can provide the foundation for self-motivation.[1]

The experiment involved a group of 120 young women who handled complaints from customers. The women were made directly responsible for deciding how the complaints should be handled and for composing their own replies. The work became a challenge, more meaningful and interesting, and provided a greater sense of fulfillment. The experiment was highly successful. Turnover and absentee rates declined; productivity increased; promotions were given; costs were reduced; and the quality of work, morale, and attitudes improved. The women were excited about their "new" jobs. This experiment indicated that work can be one of the most significant factors in stimulating self-motivation. This confirms the belief held by behavioral scientists that external motivational efforts have only limited effects on actual job performance. In most instances, external influences focus on the "maintenance efforts" and not the internal generating efforts that result in a permanent or continuing extra push.

Stimulating Her Interest

Everybody wants an interesting job, and women are no exception. But what is interesting to some people will not necessarily be interesting to others. For some, the job must be challenging and involve decision making and responsibility. For others, the job is interesting if it is important but does not involve too much responsibility. It is up to the supervisor to know each of his subordinates well enough to determine the primary interest of each and to structure and interpret the job with emphasis on each subordinate's needs. It is also up to the supervisor to know his subordinates' attitudes toward the work, the company, and himself. Without the right attitude it is doubtful that interest can be developed under any circumstances.

Job interest can be only minimal or destroyed completely when the supervisor fails to recognize good work. And poor health, the temporary nature of some work, one disgruntled member of the department, or any factor that influences the general feeling of workers will affect interest. The supervisor should highlight the interesting features of the

[1] Robert N. Ford, *Motivation Through the Work Itself* (AMA, 1969).

job and the job's overall importance in relation to the department's functions and the company's goals. He should also emphasize his own interest in the job.

Motivating Her to Work Efficiently

Motivating women to work efficiently does not mean that they must be constantly pressured to perform. It means, rather, that an effort should be made to eliminate waste — wasted motion, wasted material, and wasted time. In short, the aim of motivating women toward maximum efficiency is to make the most effective use of all available resources. In order to do this the supervisor must make certain that the work environment is what it should be. The machines, chairs and benches, and a variety of other physical factors either promote or hinder efficiency. The supervisor must also make certain that the women understand the standards of efficiency. The standard for production might be a minimum of 160 units per day. The sales standard might limit returns to 8 percent. Standards for every function should be established on a quantitative basis, and each woman should have a clear and thorough understanding of what they are.

Efficiency can be constantly improved, but only through continued training which minimizes inefficient work habits and accentuates positive job practices. It is also advisable to avoid periods of idleness since they can work against the development of efficient work habits. The work should always be scheduled to keep workers busy. The rapid, steady worker usually works more efficiently than the one who must start and stop. And the busy worker also experiences a greater sense of achievement.

The supervisor should be cognizant of the importance of pride in workmanship. How much pride does the woman have in the finished product? A job well done serves to reinforce her sense of pride, so she must be told when she has performed well. He must also remember that employees generally perform according to the expectations of their supervisor, so if he expects efficiency, he is most likely to get it.

Since employees discover very quickly what the supervisor will and will not tolerate, he should take prompt action if work continues below acceptable standards of efficiency. If inefficient work is ignored, the employee assumes it is acceptable. Inefficient performance should never be ignored. Every reasonable effort should be exerted to bring below-par work up to the acceptable standard. But if efficiency is not reached within a reasonable time, definite steps should be taken: additional training, transfer, or possibly, as a last resort, termination.

Inspiring Her Cooperation

How important is it for the supervisor to have a woman's cooperation? The importance becomes evident when analyzing the difference between cooperation and the lack of it. The cooperative worker is oriented toward trusting the supervisor's instructions and the company's policies; she has a favorable attitude, is usually well adjusted to the job, and can generally be counted on to go along with all reasonable proposals. In contrast, the uncooperative worker needs to be convinced, sometimes almost forced, to support and go along with all recommendations. She approaches most tasks with a negative attitude and performs them grudgingly. She does only what is required and seldom puts forth extra effort. She has a tendency to be suspicious of instructions and work assignments. She requires a disproportionate amount of the supervisor's time in order to get acceptable or even minimum levels of production. Cooperation can be instilled and maintained by keeping employees informed in order to minimize chances of inaccurate information causing suspicion and mistrust; by providing dependable and consistent leadership that she can trust on a continuing basis; by enabling her to get what she wants from the job and by providing satisfying working conditions; by giving thorough and appropriate instructions; and by giving constant attention to building positive attitudes.

Increasing Individual and Group Commitment

Most of this chapter has been concerned with individual motivation, and, by and large, this is where the emphasis should be placed. But the potential for group motivation must also be recognized.

Although each woman sees herself as a distinctly unique individual, she does not want to vary too much from what is acceptable within her work group. The supervisor has the opportunity to develop group standards favorable to work goals and then to influence each woman so that she meets the group norm. The ongoing patterns, attitudes, behavior, or dress of the group will have a significant influence on the commitment of each woman in the group and on those who seek acceptance from the group.

Competition as a Motivator

Contests and most other forms of competition provide motivation for increased production, sales, and safety. Women want to be winners and to be admired by their peers. Competition has the potential of stimulating interest, extra effort, greater commitment, and better results, but it is not without disadvantages. If it goes beyond certain points, hostility and negative reactions will develop.

"Winner take all" contests are not ideally suited to women. Few winners and many losers work against high morale. Contests designed primarily for women should provide for as many winners as possible. Prizes such as stamps or points that everyone can earn toward gifts are effective.

Contests and all other forms of competition should be structured to appeal to women. The competitive situation can stimulate interest and excitement and produce that extra effort, but each employee should be able to experience winning. It is better to have a woman try to beat her own production record rather than those of her fellow workers. Involve women in the makeup of contests and forms of competition that include them. Competition is a useful motivational tool; but like most management tools, it must be used discriminatingly to achieve the desired results.

Motivation and Participation

As managers continue to try to motivate their women subordinates, they will use as many approaches as they can find which they think will provide some measure of success. No one has found the perfect method, but the search continues. One of the newer methods is motivation through involvement and participation. This method, when properly used, can substantially improve motivation, especially self-motivation.

It is psychologically valid that people will have a strong commitment toward something they have helped to create themselves. Supervisors should make every effort to actively involve women in all areas that will affect them. This can be done by asking their opinions, seeking their ideas, asking for their solutions to a problem, appointing them to serve on committees, and keeping them fully informed of what is taking place.

Motivation: A Continuing Leadership Imperative

Motivation provides the unique opportunity of using women's potential for their own benefit, as well as for the benefit of the company.

The keys to motivating women are basically the same as those used to motivate all people and groups: discovering their needs and tailoring the elements of the job to meet them. It can be assumed that responsive commitment and effort will be directly related to the degree the needs are satisfied.

Women, like everyone else, will respond to appropriately designed motivational efforts. But in all instances the efforts must be sincere, honest, and beneficial for the women involved. False flattery, schemes, obvious manipulation, and cheap gimmicks will always fail and will probably jeopardize future motivational efforts.

In sum, motivating women does not involve glittering packages of promises or veiled threats of disaster. There is nothing mysterious about it. It recognizes that most women are sincere and honest. It assumes that women have basic needs and desires that the job environment is capable of fulfilling. It is based on the belief that the company can meet these needs through its leadership, its policies and practices, its ability to create a favorable work environment, and its success in treating everyone as a unique individual. Favorable results are directly related to the extent to which the company and its various levels of supervision are able to supply these job satisfiers. Women can indeed be motivated, and this benefits both the woman and the functional goals of the company.

10

Analyzing Performance: A Basis for Growth

A typical company spends approximately 60 percent of its entire operating budget for the sole purpose of buying human time. It becomes, therefore, an economic necessity to look at the block of time involved and determine how much is being contributed to the company for the money it is paying out. This evaluation becomes useful as a basis for rewarding contribution, for providing job satisfaction and recognition, and for identifying opportunities for future improvement. From a human standpoint, each woman is entitled to an accounting of her progress — how well she is doing in relation to what is expected of her — and to receive the maximum assistance from her supervisor in achieving job growth.

Reluctance to Confront Uncertainty

The thought of evaluating the job performance of women disturbs many supervisors who have to do the reviewing and the women who will be reviewed. To the woman, it involves criticism of herself and her work. To the supervisor, it involves possible confrontation with hostility. Under typical circumstances and in most companies, the practice of merit or job performance review is highly controversial and often of questionable value. There are many who claim that it does more damage to morale and existing relationships than good in the form of improved job performance. But it is possible to devise a technique that will meet the obvious need for appraisals, and, at the same time, be acceptable to and welcomed by all participants. It is hoped that this chapter will provide such a program.

THE JOINT VENTURE APPROACH

The joint-venture-for-future-job-growth method requires a form of the kind illustrated in Figure 2. A study of this form will provide an understanding of the program. Typically, a large company will need to develop a number and variety of forms in order to cover all the major duties and responsibilities in every category of work. Most companies need forms specially adapted for production workers, supervisors, executives, clerks, sales people, and others, depending on the nature of the company. Joint venture is not a stereotyped program; but the form, the review, the program for growth, and the interview should always be structured to meet the specific growth needs of the person being reviewed.

The joint venture form should always contain an indication of the employee's present performance as a foundation for building a realistic program for future job growth. (This is achieved by circling the appro-

Figure 2
Joint Venture for Future Job Growth
(Supervisor/Employee)

Date_____

Name _____ Position and department _____
Location _____ No. _____ City _____
Date hired _____ Birth date _____
Date of last interview_____ Date assumed present position _____

REVIEW FACTORS—GOALS FOR GROWTH

Performance Levels

Circle the number in each box below that represents the individual's present performance in this area.

1 *Below standard:* Is not meeting minimum requirements and standards of position.
2 *Satisfactory:* Meets requirements and standards of position.
3 *Outstanding:* Exceeds requirements and standards of position.

Goals and Growth

Be as specific as possible in setting goals and standards, and in developing the program for their achievement. Qualify with $'s, %'s, amounts, dates, methods, changes, etc. Relate to this position and this individual. (Use and attach additional sheets, if necessary.)

PRESENT PERFORMANCE	PROGRAM FOR ACHIEVING GOALS AND GROWTH
Knowledge of job: Understands job. Applies knowledge in an effective manner. Able to function with normal supervision. (Refer to Position Description.) 1 2 3	
Quality of work: Work is accurate, legible, and well done. Works according to established company methods. 1 2 3	
Quantity of work: Output compares with standards set for the job or with performance of associates in similar jobs. Completes assignments in allotted time. 1 2 3	
Customer service: (Where applicable.) Is enthusiastic and gracious in manner. Helpful in solving customer problems. 1 2 3	
Attitude: Cooperates with and helps other employees and supervisors. Interested in job. Adjusts to changes in systems and procedures. Complies with regulations. 1 2 3	
Appearance and personality: Maintains high standards of personal grooming. Conforms to company dress regulations. Maintains harmonious relations with others. 1 2 3	

Present Performance	Program for Achieving Goals and Growth
Initiative: Assumes responsibility. Is alert to methods of improving work. Requires minimum supervision in performance of work. 1 2 3	_____ _____ _____ _____ _____
Dependability: Is reliable in following work schedules and assignments. Is punctual; has good attendance record. Follows through and completes assignments. 1 2 3	_____ _____ _____ _____ _____

Total number 1s _____ 2s _____ 3s _____

Interviewer's Evaluation

Strong points: (Personal attributes that have enabled or will enable the employee to make significant contributions to his job performance.)

Areas for improvement: (Areas in which improvements can and should be made.)

Employee's Remarks

Employee's comments and plans: (The employee should indicate his or her own observations and future plans for personal growth.)

Supervisor/employee joint program for future job growth: (What experience, training, job rotation, etc. is planned during the next 12 months to assist this employee in attaining additional job growth? Indicate the approximate dates of planned programs. If necessary, attach an additional sheet to specify goals and objectives agreed on for the next 12 months.)

_____   _____
       Employer's signature   Date of interview

priate number on the form.) It must also provide for the establishment of specific growth goals and an individualized program for achieving these goals. (The form includes this under the heading "Program for Achieving Goals and Growth.")

An interview should result in the supervisor and the employee agreeing on present performance levels, developing a program for future growth, and committing themselves to whatever offers the greatest potential for performance improvement.

Immediately after the joint discussion, the interviewer should note on the back of the form his opinions about the employee's qualifications for promotion. Is she ready for it now? If so, what job would be best? If she is not ready, approximately how long will it be before she can be considered for a promotion? The interviewer might also wish to add some comments about the long-range potential of the employee and any other observations.

The weaknesses of traditional job performance evaluation programs stem from the resentment they cause in those being evaluated. These programs imply a criticism that is psychologically unacceptable. The focus is too much on past performance — yesterday's hits or errors — something that neither the supervisor nor the employee can do anything about now. The joint venture approach, on the other hand, focuses on the past only as a basis for building for the future. It is a review of performance and achievement rather than of expectations that might or might not be fulfilled. Nor does it compare one person with another; it measures each worker's performance against her own specific responsibilities and objectives.

The review must be a positive experience. The woman must believe that the company and the supervisor are vitally concerned with her future job growth and that they are willing to work with her to bring it about.

The joint venture approach thus becomes a shared responsibility of the supervisor and the employee. It involves united action, development of common goals, a mutual undertaking, and shared risks and rewards.

Joint venture provides a predictable and systematic basis for mutual understanding and communication. Thus, the all-important need for an objective and impersonal relationship is created through day-to-day interaction and progress toward mutually agreed-upon expectations. It is a frame of reference through which both supervisor and subordinate can identify and expand their job efforts. Such a process meets the needs of both the women and the company. A woman's needs are met because she knows where she stands in relation to her progress, her achievement, and her future opportunities; she is provided with job satisfaction in the form of recognition and approval of praiseworthy performance; she is given the opportunity to be heard, to participate, to present her side, and to be involved; she is provided with an individually structured program designed to maximize her full potential for growth; and she receives the opportunity to discuss openly her job performance and future growth with the company.

Of first priority in the review is the identification of all the elements of the job and how performance of these elements relates to job success. In other words, What must be done, and how well? A written job description would be useful in this respect, since it enables the supervisor and the woman to see the job in the same way.

Once the responsibilities and duties of the job have been clarified, the next step is to determine whether normal performance standards are being met. (See Figure 2 under "Performance Levels" for rating scale.)

The supervisor must then spell out, in quantitative terms, exactly what goal expectations and standards of performance are. He must explain exactly what "below standard," "satisfactory," and "outstanding" mean in relation to the specific job in question. This might be easily determined on the production line, but is more difficult to define for a bank teller or creative artist. But even when difficulties arise, the supervisor and subordinate should continue working toward quantitative objectivity until they agree on what constitutes satisfactory performance.

Now that standards have been set, supervisor and subordinate face the problem of deciding whether the subordinate's performance has met the standards. If standards of performance have never been discussed or mutually agreed upon before, this can be a sticky problem. However, now that desired standards are clearly understood, arguments or disagreements about what might have been are senseless. This problem points up the importance of open communication and the value of joint planning. If desired standards are set and understood, there can be little disagreement on levels of performance.

Even though clearly defined standards are essential to job performance, some flexibility must be maintained. Women will generally work more effectively if they have enough latitude to use their own methods and judgment, which in the long run may prove superior to those recommended by the supervisor. This is not to suggest that the range of flexibility is so great that results become seriously threatened. But if a woman has a feeling of maneuverability and freedom, and of being respected enough to be allowed some independence and initiative within the confines of the job, she will probably exceed expectations and justify the faith placed in her.

When the supervisor begins designing the program for growth on the job, it would be well worth his while to remember to focus on the future; concentrate on job activity, not on personalities; aim to develop, not to discipline; encourage progress and eliminate any roadblocks that may stand in the way; treat the woman as an individual; relate her development and growth to goals and standards; and be objective, factual, and specific.

The supervisor must communicate his willingness to make reasonable changes in supervision and in the work environment if such changes will promote performance improvement. He should also indicate that the resources of the company are available to help her with her development. The following checklist might be useful for insuring that he has clarified —

> What is expected of this woman in this job?
> Where should her emphasis be placed?
> What specific goals should be set for her?
> What are desirable or undesirable job-related activities?

Although the supervisor has expended a lot of time and effort in developing a program for his subordinate's future growth, nothing is really accomplished until the interview. The purpose of the interview is to communicate and implement the program. The following guides are suggested for conducting an effective interview.

Preparation and planning. The supervisor should be able to justify the rating given to the woman's present job performance; have production, attendance, and other information available as supporting evidence of performance; provide her with a sense of recognition and satisfaction; review in advance possible problem areas in which he anticipates the greatest difficulty in reaching agreement on present performance level or on specifics for future growth; try to build a better relationship with her by clarifying mutual objectives.

The interview itself. The supervisor should immediately clarify the purpose of the interview and establish rapport; give her an opportunity to ask questions and make comments; avoid putting her on the defensive by minimizing discussions of past performance or anything that could be interpreted as personal criticism rather than constructive guidance; give her ample opportunity to explain obstacles or hindrances that she has confronted in the past or feels she will meet in her future growth efforts; welcome her opinions and be willing to listen to what she has to say; explain very carefully, and in as much detail as necessary, goals and activities regarding her opportunity for future job growth.

The supervisor should then *conclude* with as complete an agreement as possible on present performance levels, future changes, specific goals, and expected growth.

He then creates a basis for *future rapport* and assures her of the company's continuing interest in her future job growth.

It is essential for the supervisor to *follow through* with meaningful, daily interaction.

Remember that the formal review cannot be expected to take the place of daily supervisory responsibilities. The formal review, the program for future job growth, and the interview should only summarize the constant working relationship of the supervisor and the subordinate. It is an illusion to assume that performance improvement can be attained through a once-a-year or even a twice-a-year conversation. Although the formal review has value for both the supervisor and the subordinate, it should never be expected to achieve the goals that must be identified, strengthened, and continuously reinforced daily.

Both the formal program and the daily relationship should focus on opportunities for improvement. It is the future that provides the opportunity for the woman to make the job contribution both she and her supervisor desire. Women welcome the opportunity to talk about future improvement opportunities. The direction of attention on mutual goals and expectations is psychologically acceptable to women. And they will appreciate the supervisor's interest and welcome his assistance.

The primary purpose of reviewing job performance should be to change the woman's future job behavior in a positive way. The review should motivate her to look at her work objectively with a view to changing habits and attitudes that are ineffective or disruptive in the work environment. The benefits it reaps must be measured in terms of how much desirable change really occurs immediately and on a continuing basis.

The woman on the job wants and needs assistance for improving her job performance. If she receives it from the proper sources, and it is appropriately structured for her own needs, she will accept it, respond to it, and improve on the job. The formal review and the day-to-day appraisal, correction, encouragement, and job development provide the supervisor with vast opportunities for improving the performance of and results achieved by women. Both the formal review and daily supervision can make a significant contribution to the growth of women on the job and to the company.

11

Molding
and Guiding Attitudes

IF you can mold an employee's attitude, you can shape her future job performance. It is doubtful that any other factor exerts so strong an influence as does attitude — whether it is the supervisor's or the subordinate's. Favorable attitudes can make the job a pleasant and satisfying experience; negative and antagonistic attitudes can stymie the whole process. Positive attitudes can eliminate problems; negative ones create problems. Attitudes determine whether a woman is a willing contributor or holds back and is a detriment to the whole team.

Understanding Women's Attitudes

A woman's attitudes control her reactions to the people and environment around her. Her attitudes tell her whether to trust her boss and whether he deserves her loyal cooperation, support, and best effort. If attitude is rigidly set, then additional information, logic, different circumstances or facts that may prove her wrong are not likely to alter her attitudes. Women may prefer to let themselves be guided by their emotions rather than by facts. Thus, when a woman's beliefs, her interpretation of circumstances, and her responses are based on strong feelings, changes in supervision, company policies, or the original justification for the formation of her attitude will have little effect on her. Obviously, such behavior and reactions are totally inappropriate to the work environment.

This inflexible posture presents special handicaps for both the supervisor and the woman on the job. It prevents them both from seeing or reacting to the dictates of new situations as they arise. There have been many instances where attitudes were more decisive than circumstances in determining behavior. Take the example of Helen Davenport, who was one of eight employees in a department where there was a shortage of money. An investigation involved all eight employees in the department. When the source of the shortage was discovered, Mrs. Davenport was not implicated in any way. This was explained to her, and her supervisor apologized for the inconvenience, stating the reasons for having to check out everyone in the department. But she so bitterly resented the idea that the company could even remotely consider her dishonest that she insisted on a transfer and refused to be involved in the handling of money after that time. No amount of apologizing or explaining could change her mind.

The challenge to the supervisor is that he must cope with emotionally charged situations where facts do not always determine reactions. In some instances a woman may be reacting to or forming attitudes about something that happened to her before she ever started working for the company. "All companies give their employees as little as they can get away with. Whenever I wanted something from a company, I've had to either beg or threaten them. So I expect the same thing here." An employee who talks like this is certainly going to be a problem for her supervisor. He must first identify what has caused such a negative attitude before he can begin to cope with it.

A supervisor once remarked, "Jane's attitude is terrible. She can't get along with anyone in the department. She's always causing trouble, and she refuses to cooperate. I know something must be done, but I don't look forward to talking with her about it. I know she's going to blow sky high. Talking with a woman about her attitude is asking for trouble." This is a fairly typical comment and it is not completely unjustified. The mere use of the word "attitude" implies an undesirable condition, which she might be unwilling to admit exists, and a criticism of how she feels, which is, after all, a personal matter. The typical association with "attitude" is negative. Seldom does a supervisor compliment a woman on her favorable attitude. Usually, a favorable attitude is referred to in other terms such as cooperation, support, or loyalty.

When a supervisor discusses an attitude with a female subordinate, he should focus on the need for cooperation with others, how it affects her work, the present and future benefits of recommended changes, and any other factors directly related to the job.

The Supervisor's Attitudes: A Decisive Starting Point

Attitudes have a way of becoming more visible than might be desired. Women are extremely perceptive and can detect attitudes more readily than men. They also resent the supervisor who expresses negative attitudes regarding women in business or who frequently mentions women's shortcomings, his lack of confidence in women, or his attitude toward a particular woman. A woman will probably be more aware of the nature and depth of his attitude than he is.

The attitude a woman adopts is often a reflection of the attitude the supervisor exhibits in his relationship with her. If this is one of trust, confidence, and cooperation, she will probably form the same kind of attitude in working with him.

If the supervisor clings to basically untrue notions about women, such as that they have physical limitations, are frail and easily fatigued, cannot stand noise, dirt, or drafts, and have to go to the washroom too frequently, his attitude will show through and will be easily recognized. Clichés of this kind are usually one part truth and nine parts nonsense, but they are difficult to uproot. For example, an auto manufacturer defended the exclusion of women from his industry with the explanation that women aren't able to stand up to the stresses and strains of the business world even though the evidence is clear that men, not women, succumb to ulcers and heart attacks. Or take the case of a consumer goods manufacturer who said that it isn't within the makeup of most men to acknowledge that the female business mind is equal to their own despite the fact that numerous women have proved to be very successful in business. In a survey of co-workers and supervisors, the U.S. Civil Service Commission reports that most negative attitudes concerning women workers are held by men who have had little or no experience in working with women. However, 45 percent of men who had extensive experience in working with both sexes reported that they could detect no difference between the job performance of men and women.

The Influence of Attitudes

Just how significant and far-reaching is the influence of women's attitudes? A female bookkeeper was required to work closely with a male accountant. She recalls, "He was foul-mouthed and one of the most obnoxious individuals I have ever had to work with. I had to constantly be on my guard regarding what he said and what he was doing. I finally had such a negative attitude toward him that it became almost impossible to work with him. I believed that everything he was doing was wrong. I suppose I expected it to be wrong. If I was late in the morning, rushed, or not feeling well, I just knew that working with him that day would be a catastrophe — and it usually was. Yes, I knew what was happening, but my attitude was so negative about him and everything he represented that it just about ruined my chances of working effectively with him."

A female administrative assistant remarked, in speaking of one employee, "Look, she doesn't stay at her desk. She spends half her time making personal calls. Don't think for a minute that I'm going to do her work. In fact, I don't want to have anything to do with her. Least of all, I don't want to be blamed for what she doesn't get done or have to pick up the pieces for her."

If strong emotional attitudes such as these are allowed to form, it can be assumed that they will have more influence on whether a woman likes her job, whether she remains on it, and how she performs while there than will any conversation with the supervisor. Developing attitudes can also be signs of "constructive discontent." If such attitudes receive the appropriate response, they can be used to increase job satisfaction and production. It is often the inspirationally dissatisfied person who causes changes to occur. The supervisor can use discontent as a tool for improvement.

The Source of Attitudes

Attitudes don't suddenly materialize on a Monday morning, neatly packaged, without cause or explanation. They might be the result of a lifetime of experiences or the result of one traumatic episode. The following paragraphs may throw some light on the understanding of attitudes.

An attitude is learned, not inherited. Infants have no inborn attitudes or preconceived opinions. Attitudes cannot be attributed to circumstances of heredity but to the learning that occurs later.

The principal source of attitudes is the environment. The attitudes a person has are the result of her physical and mental environment since birth. Just like a computer operation, the input has consisted of mostly small bits and pieces, but occasionally large, significant facts are programmed. A woman's current attitude is a reaction to her total experience.

Attitudes can be acquired from others. It is sometimes surprising how readily people will accept and adopt the attitude of someone else without stopping to examine the facts objectively. In these cases, a strong-willed or bitter member of a group can seriously affect the attitudes and thinking of all the others by imposing her attitude on them.

Attitudes may be based on only one dramatic experience. It is certainly possible for one traumatic experience to affect a person for life. If a child's favorite toy is taken away by a parent, the child may assume that all authority figures are not to be trusted, and this attitude can carry over into later life. More relevant here would be the experience of a woman who is humiliated in front of others by a supervisor. She may then develop the attitude that all supervisors are the same and will treat her the same way — such an attitude can remain fixed throughout her working life. If a supervisor is aware of the environment and the emotional experiences of his subordinates, he will be more likely to understand the source of their attitudes and be able to cope with them. Although it might not be possible to change a prevailing attitude, the supervisor's awareness of it should influence the kind of leadership he offers.

Basic Facts About Attitudes

Attitudes are not unfathomable mysteries that defy understanding. It is possible, based on known data, to anticipate the manner in which attitudes are likely to develop and what should be done to influence them in a favorable direction.

Attitudes develop quickly. One Monday morning a new girl reported to the ready-to-wear department of a large Chicago department store. She was greeted by one of the older saleswomen with the statement, "You look like a real nice girl. I can't understand why you came to work here. I'll tell you one thing — you won't like this department, and you won't be able to stand the supervisor." It isn't surprising that the new girl didn't like the department, couldn't get along with the supervisor, and left after three weeks.

First impressions are extremely significant. The most important minute, day, and week in the life of a new woman employee is the first one. She may be uncertain and impressionable. Her attitudes begin to form immediately, based on what she sees, hears, and by the way she is treated. If she is ignored, there's a good chance that she will form negative attitudes. Hence, the supervisor should welcome, orient, and help a new employee in a way that will lead her to form positive attitudes right from the start.

Attitudes are relatively permanent. It is far easier to influence the formation of an attitude than it is to change one once it is developed. While cement is still in a liquid state, it can be shaped without difficulty; but once it begins to set and becomes firm, it is almost impossible to make changes. This obviously presents a formidable challenge to the supervisor.

Attitudes are interrelated. Evelyn Sommers was one of twenty women employed in a public accounting office. She had been there for three years and was considered one of the best and most cooperative people in the group. Everyone in her department understood that no one would be given vacations during the two-month period prior to the April 15 tax deadline except in the case of an emergency. On April 2, Mrs. Sommers approached her supervisor, requesting that she be given her two-week vacation, beginning the following Monday. She knew about the rules and how busy things would be during that time. But her husband had just told her that things were slow where he worked, and his boss had suggested that he take his vacation during this time. After a lengthy discussion with her supervisor she finally agreed not to take time off. "But," she said, "my husband isn't going to like it. If you insist, I won't take my vacation now, but it won't mean much to me if I have to take it later by myself." Her attitude was never quite the same again: she became dissatisfied with her salary, had trouble with her co-workers, and had difficulty with her supervisor. Her negative attitude about the vacation incident soon spread to other areas of her work.

So we can see that if a woman has a very strong attitude regarding one area of her job, she is likely to carry over this attitude to other areas. The supervisor's awareness of the far-reaching influence of one attitude should cause him to explain his decisions and actions thoroughly, especially when he knows that they may cause pockets of discontent that can spread like cancer.

Behavior and job performance are affected by attitudes. What an employee does and achieves on the job is often directly related to her attitudes, which can cause things to happen or prevent them from happening on the job. Attitudes cause her to exert maximum effort or to try to get by with the minimum.

Attitude formation is different for different people. A supervisor shouldn't expect every woman in the department to respond in the same way to his attempts at attitude influence; they won't. He must remember that each has been conditioned by her own unique environment and must be supervised with this in mind.

Developing Favorable Attitudes

The point here is to mold the initial attitude development of women. It is at the beginning of employment that the supervisor has the best opportunity to exert a significant influence. His efforts should be carefully planned, systematic, and continuing. He should:

• Make certain that her initial impression is positive and favorable. The supervisor's greeting should be warm, friendly, and sincere. A strong, well-planned orientation procedure will aid in the development of favorable attitudes.

• Accept responsibility for her attitude development, at least the portion that will be shaped on the job. The supervisor cannot afford to assume that satisfactory attitudes will develop in the normal course of events.

• Create and maintain a climate conducive to favorable attitude development. It should be one in which promises are kept, consideration given, trust exhibited, confidence expressed, assistance made available, and courtesy extended. It is one that can only stem from the supervisor's positive attitudes. He must demonstrate confidence in her ability and the probability of her success.

• Provide all the information she needs for positive attitude formation. Her attitudes will be based on the knowledge available to her. If it is inaccurate or insufficient, her attitudes will reflect this. The supervisor's positive approach involves ample initial and continuing communication with her.

• Avoid surprises by letting her know exactly what to expect. If she doesn't know what to anticipate, she might expect the worst. And if she does, she will build up defenses against the unknown. The supervisor must make it clear to her that he will tell her about everything that might affect her or her job. She will develop an attitude of trust, confidence, and cooperation if she knows what to expect.

• Make the work itself a favorable influence on her attitude. Initial work assignments and requirements should be within the limitations of her experience and present capabilities. The supervisor must insure that she has an adequate understanding of how the work is to be done, how well it should be done, and the results expected. He should make her feel that her performance is acceptable by recognizing her progress and praising her achievements.

• Make certain that her peer group contributes to the development of favorable attitudes. If she is skeptical of the company's motives or the methods of supervisors, she might be influenced more by her co-workers than by her supervisors. It is a safe bet that within a few months of reporting for work she will have adopted many of the attitudes that prevailed in the department before she arrived.

It is certainly easier to mold new attitudes than to change old ones. As has already been mentioned, attitudes are relatively permanent, so that the difficulty lies in changing strong feelings rather than facts. By the time a supervisor becomes aware that a change in attitude is called for, a woman's attitude has become familiar and acceptable to her and she feels comfortable with it. So why should she change? Why accept the unfamiliar? The woman will not change until she recognizes that her attitude is wrong or that a change will better meet her needs.

Regardless of the supervisor's elaborate care with new female employees and his attention to co-workers, unfavorable attitudes often emerge. It is at this stage that the supervisor cannot ignore their potential harm. He must now try to change them.

He should attempt to replace an undesirable attitude with a desirable one. The small child will hold on to a dangerous object until he is offered a more desirable one. It is virtually impossible to eliminate an attitude and leave nothing in its place. The substitute should serve the needs of the woman more beneficially.

The supervisor can point out the disadvantages of his subordinate's behavior. If she objects to working for a woman, for example, and feels that all women supervisors are unfair, he should ask her why she feels this way. He can point out that if she were to become a supervisor, she would not want other women to feel the same way. She should have plenty of time to discuss her feelings and should be made to see how they work to her detriment. He should ask her to consider alternatives and point out their advantages and benefits to her. She must have acceptable reasons for making the change.

He should ask for only a small change at first and not count on her willingness to make a dramatic change all at once. Big changes create anxiety, but changes made one small step at a time provide continuing security. Although a subordinate might feel perfectly justified in not wanting to make a major change, she can see that she is less justified in refusing to make a small one. This might mean gradually removing undesirable grains of sand from one side of the attitude scales.

It might be worthwhile for the supervisor to ask for agreement to a trial change. Would she refuse merely to try cooperating with a co-worker who has been causing her trouble? Probably not if all that's asked for is cooperation. And she doesn't have to *like* her co-worker. All she has to do is agree to work with her so that the department will not suffer.

It is possible that a worker's attitude is based on a limited understanding of the total picture of the job. If she doesn't understand what the supervisor is trying to achieve when he changes work assignments, increases her workload, or denies her certain privileges, she is not likely to change her attitude.

If and when the supervisor finally does bring about a change in attitude, he must take care that the subordinate does not revert to her old ways. He should see to it that the changes she's made are satisfying and beneficial to her. He should use the changes as motivation for even more changes. Once the trend is under way and the desired change achieved, she should be complimented for her cooperation and job improvement and reminded of how she has benefited. The supervisor must keep promises that might have been made as an inducement to make the change.

Maintaining a Favorable Climate for Positive Attitudes

The supervisor should remember these five key factors as he seeks to create and maintain favorable attitudes:

1. Attitudes have an important influence on both the quantity and the quality of her work.

2. Attitudes affect job satisfaction, length of employment, and the amount of supervision required.

3. Attitudes are influenced by a wide variety of past experiences and factors in the present work environment.

4. Attitudes can best be channeled in favorable directions by controlling those factors that influence attitudes. This must be done without any hint of manipulation or undue control.

5. Favorable attitudes are the result of the supervisor's sincerity as well as his own favorable attitudes. He must be what he seems to be. He must give substantial reasons why she should feel and react in a way that will be most beneficial to her own best interests and to those of the company.

Undoubtedly women with unfavorable attitudes do some work and are often permitted to remain on the job. But supervising such employees is like trying to drive a car with the brakes on. It is to the supervisor's and employee's self-interests to work jointly toward developing the best attitudes possible. Attitude development is too critical to be ignored or left to chance, and its maintenance is the supervisor's responsibility. Women expect him to provide the positive direction.

12

Hazards and Opportunities in Discipline and Correction

SOME women tend to react very emotionally to criticism. They might even take advantage of their show of emotion to make their supervisors reluctant to discipline or correct them at all. Any supervisor who has had the experience of an overly emotional woman exploding at him because of his criticism will certainly think twice before he says anything to her again. He might even assume, although incorrectly, that all women react that way—that they just can't take criticism.

Correction of employee job performance is unavoidable in every leadership position. The coach who is willing to incur the displeasure of his players corrects performance and wins ballgames. The parent guides his child toward maturity through corrective action not because it is pleasant, but because it serves the best interests of both parent and child.

Yet in spite of the obvious need for it, correction is the most mis-understood, neglected, and delayed supervisory responsibility—especially where women are concerned. It is neglected because the supervisor might not have confidence in his ability to handle it correctly and is afraid of negative feedback. Or he may overreact and verbally pounce on the woman because of her shortcomings. She, in turn, will naturally feel resentful and mistreated. If a supervisor believes that his primary function is to stage a popularity contest and be a "good guy," he is likely to let mistakes go unnoticed, to settle for below-par production standards, and to be content with halfhearted cooperation. The result is an inevitable loss of respect and a breakdown of productivity. Yet somewhere out of the morass of uncertainty, the supervisor has to distinguish between "too little" and "too much."

Correction: A Unique Opportunity

Thoreau stated that "man was born to succeed, not to fail." It can be assumed that the woman worker wants to succeed, that she wants to do her job well, and that if given a choice between satisfactory and unsatisfactory job performance, she will choose the approved course. Correction should be viewed as the supervisor's unique opportunity to render a service to his employee so that she will be able to succeed in her job. To illustrate this point, a supervisor could say to his subordinate what this supervisor said to his female bookkeeper. "Mrs. Nelson, I believe you've been here about five years. But frankly, I'm now concerned about your work. I know that you want to handle the invoices correctly and get them out on time, but lately you haven't been keeping to the schedule we agreed on. If we don't do something to correct the situation, I'm afraid that one of these days we'll have to consider making a change. Now, what I'm most concerned about is how we can work together to meet the schedule and send out the invoices correctly. I want to see you stay on the job because I've enjoyed working with you, and I know that you can do the work."

If a supervisor ignores unsatisfactory work until his employee resigns in disgust or is discharged, both he and the employee suffer. But by making every reasonable effort to correct her job performance, thereby improving her job security and her chances for success, the supervisor is benefiting everyone. So an employee who is permitted to continue unsatisfactory job performance is being given unfair and inappropriate leadership.

There are two basic kinds of discipline—preventive and corrective. An annual physical checkup by the doctor is preventive medicine; medication to reduce fever is corrective medicine. Preventive medicine and preventive discipline are preferable to corrective medicine or discipline. Preventive discipline teaches correct job habits and practices, provides an understanding of rules, insures sufficient knowledge and motivation to enable the woman to engage in self-discipline and control, and prevents the need for corrective discipline. However, if corrective discipline becomes necessary, the supervisor should try to reestablish as quickly as possible the proper climate for preventive discipline.

Perhaps the single most important fact the supervisor needs to understand about correcting a woman is the opportunity he is giving her to increase her job security, her chances for promotion, and her compensation opportunities. However, in order to accomplish this, he must get her to understand the purpose of correction and how it may be used to fulfill her job-related needs.

Correction also works to the self-interest of the supervisor. He cannot meet the standards required of his department unless each person is doing her fair share. Most of his supervisory and training problems stem from incorrect job performance, so once this can be corrected, his own chances for success are greatly improved. The greater the time lapse between the beginning of unsatisfactory job performance and its correction, the greater the loss will be to the goals of the department.

Understanding the Need for Correction

Why is correction necessary? The need for correction arises when the required standards of the job are not being met. Then and only then is correction justified. It is assumed that the manner in which the job should be done has been explained to the woman, that she has been trained, and that she is capable of performing what is expected of her. However, sometimes no prerequisites have been established and such gaps cause unsatisfactory work. The need for correction can best be viewed in the following context:

Standards of job performance exist. When the job is being performed in accordance with expectations, there is no need for correction.

When the woman fails to meet set standards, correction is necessary. Her failure can be sins of omission or commission: the failure to do the things required by the job or by engaging in job performance or behavior that is detrimental to the purposes of the job.

Correction should not be personal criticism, but a restoration of required job performance. Changing job performance is much easier than trying to change a woman's nature.

This understanding of correction makes it more objective and acceptable to the woman involved, and certainly more palatable for the supervisor to handle.

To avoid problems both the supervisor and the employee should agree at the outset that job performance will be considered satisfactory when certain specific standards are met and that correction will become necessary when those standards are not met.

Performance Correction versus Personal Criticism

Some supervisors fear that a woman will take job correction as personal criticism, since it might be difficult for her to separate performance correction from personal criticism. She may view correction of her work as a reflection on her personally, and therefore resent it. A supervisor's correction interviews should generally run something like this:

"Mrs. Lambert, everyone in the department certainly likes you. Only last week, it came to my attention that a customer had complimented you on your courtesy. I wish everyone around here had your personality. However, the reason I asked you to come by for a talk today is that we need to discuss your production. This, of course, does not reflect on you personally; but we must talk about your work. As you know, your job has certain production standards, and the records show that you are not meeting them. We need to discuss ways for you to meet these standards. But please remember that we're not talking about you personally, only about job results."

The purpose of this approach is to keep the woman from letting the conversation about the work become a personal issue. It is wise to keep reminding her that it is the work and not the individual that is being discussed. A woman's acceptance of correction depends almost entirely on the manner in which the supervisor handles the situation.

A young executive pointed out to a clerical worker that some of the figures on her weekly report were wrong. She then emitted a stifled sob, slammed the door, and ran down the hall. This only added to his frustration. "But I only pointed out to her that some of the figures were wrong. I guess I just don't understand women," the executive told an associate. The executive is obviously evading the issue. Blaming the "eternal feminine mystique" is no remedy for his problem. His criticism might have been too abrupt. He should have made his comments in private, and he should have started the conversation by recognizing her favorable personality traits or the good features of her job performance. If no attention is given to the positive aspects of her work, then she assumes that the supervisor is not aware of any or, worse, that he sees only what she has done wrong.

Do women tend to take correction more personally than men? In a survey conducted by Edgar S. Ellman, almost three out of four executives (both men and women) answered "yes." "While it has been known for some time that the so-called personal approach works best in any type of disciplinary situation, the survey indicates that careful consideration of the facts and special techniques are needed in order to motivate a woman employee to improve through discipline." [1]

The difficulty women have in disassociating job correction from personal criticism constitutes the greatest hazard the supervisor confronts in his correction of women. He feels competent to talk to her about her job performance and job-related activity, but is not able to handle personal, emotional reactions. She doesn't deliberately try to make it difficult for him; but she considers her job performance a personal matter.

The supervisor finds himself in a quandary: He cannot ignore inefficiency and unsatisfactory job performance; but, if he acts to correct the situation, he may be running the risk of making matters worse — and possibly embarrassing himself with his superiors. A department manager held a correction interview with a cashier who was not following the written company policy. She resigned in a huff, stating, "The very idea of thinking that I'm dishonest when I am doing things exactly the way everyone else does them. It's insulting." The following morning she was waiting to see the president when he came in. She reported, "I've been embarrassed and mistreated. I was merely doing what everyone else in the department was doing, apparently with the knowledge and approval of the department manager." The woman was wrong, and the president supported the supervisor; but the supervisor was at fault for allowing lax practices to exist in his department. The supervisor has to be overly cautious in order to focus on the objective aspects of job performance and must keep attention away from all personal inferences.

PROCEDURES FOR CORRECTION

How does the supervisor approach the task of correction of women? Three of the most typical reactions are lack of self-confidence and timidity, or overaggressiveness, or an overemphasis on the need to be popular.

Consider these six guides as aids for effective and acceptable correction:

The supervisor's own attitude and understanding of the purpose of correction is decisive. It is not his duty to punish, browbeat, embarrass, belittle, or criticize personalities. His only purpose is to make an ob-

[1] *Managing Women in Business* (Waterford, Conn.: National Foreman's Institute. 1967).

jective analysis of job performance and seek correction of faulty performance or activities when necessary.

The supervisor should never correct or discipline in the presence of others. This is simply a matter of common courtesy and consideration. A woman supervisor remarked about her boss, "He can say almost anything he wants about how I do my job . . . in the privacy of his office. But he'd better not say anything in front of the other supervisors or when any of my people are around."

The supervisor should never attempt to correct a woman when either he or she is upset or angry. Timing is all important. Calm objectivity is the rule. A favorable result is impossible if either the supervisor or the subordinate is emotional about what has happened. Unless it is an emergency or involves an immediate potential danger, correction can wait until both calm down.

The supervisor must never correct before he knows all the facts. He can be terribly embarrassed to learn that he has attempted to correct a problem that does not exist.

The supervisor should beware of hearsay. He is constantly bombarded with hints, gossip, and innuendos of what is going on.

The supervisor of a major wholesale division came rushing into the personnel department and stated, "You've got to get Mrs. Stalling out of my department — today. She's disrupting the whole department. The fact that she's an assistant supervisor would make you think that she knows better." The facts, as later revealed, indicated that the supervisor's secretary was the bearer of the tales about Mrs. Stalling. When the supervisor was out of town, the secretary had been keeping detailed notes on everything she thought was going on in the department and reported these, along with her own biased interpretation, to the supervisor when he returned. The supervisor should have verified the facts himself before recommending such drastic action.

The supervisor should not delay correction when it is clearly needed. The old adage about an ounce of prevention being worth a pound of cure is good advice when applied to the correction of faulty habits, attitudes, and work procedures. The longer correction is delayed, the more entrenched a practice becomes, and the more difficult it is to dislodge.

A bank vice-president was reviewing the work of a department with the department's supervisor. In the course of the review, the supervisor revealed that one reason for not getting the work out on time was that several of the women were late every morning. When asked what he had done about the situation, the supervisor replied that he hesitated to be too hard on the women because they normally did a good job, and he didn't want to upset them. He finally admitted that lateness had "sort of become a habit" in the department. He was instructed to correct the situation. During the process, one of the women resigned because correction had been delayed so long that habits had become firmly entrenched, and she felt that she was suddenly being picked on.

Correction, like any other management technique, should always be handled with skill and finesse, whether men or women are being corrected. Although a supervisor should not rush pell-mell into correction, neither should he delay or ignore what is clearly a part of his supervisory responsibility.

Conducting Correction Interviews

The most important aspect of the whole correction process is the correction interview. After adequate preparation and analysis of the situation, the supervisor should be ready to interview the woman. He should:

Prepare carefully for the interview. The location should provide privacy, and sufficient time should be available for the interview to proceed without interruption. Any interview that is interrupted or has to be conducted on a piecemeal basis is seldom effective, and in the case of correction interviews, interruptions can only add to the difficulties involved. He must also try to arrange for the woman to be out of her department at a time when her absence will be least conspicuous.

Plan in advance how the interview will be handled. It is often advisable for the supervisor to write down pertinent facts and information and have a clear concept of what there is about this individual's job activity that constitutes unsatisfactory job performance. He can consider various ways the correction can be made. The supervisor should be in charge of the interview, should direct its course, and should never lose control of it. Even though he has an interview plan, he should be prepared to make some adjustments as the interview proceeds. And if he keeps the overall problem in mind, he is less likely to become embroiled in emotional controversy.

Begin with a question. The woman should feel that her supervisor is open-minded and willing to hear what she has to say. If he launches into a long, emotional tirade the moment she enters the room, this can cause trouble. A good opening question might be, "How do you think your work is going?"

Link praise with criticism. The woman must be doing something right. A young stenographer offended her company vice-president by calling him by his first name. The problem was solved when her supervisor called her in and complimented her on the excellent job she was doing. He then told her that many new employees made the mistake of calling a top executive by his first name and suggested that "we all feel he deserves to be called 'Mr.' out of respect for his position." Some praise and recognition should precede the criticism. The "sandwich" technique is often effective. The supervisor can begin with praise, discuss the correction required, and end with praise.

Listen to what she has to say. Often she is justified and cannot do the work differently because of uncontrollable circumstances. The supervisor must listen carefully with an open mind and be willing to consider what she has to say and to change the nature of the planned correction if necessary.

Try to agree on the basic information and facts. It is up to the supervisor to make certain that he and the employee are both talking about the same thing. Does she agree that the production standard is 26 units an hour and that her current level averages only 21 units? Does she agree that she has failed to call in when absent three times during the past month, even though she knows that she is supposed to call in by 9:30? When agreement has been reached, attention can then be given to correction.

Keep the interview impersonal. The woman should be reminded that this is not a review or discussion of her personally. The supervisor can do this by keeping the discussion on the objective facts surrounding job performance.

Keep company policies and practices in mind. Before the interview, the supervisor should seek advice from superiors or staff people if it seems advisable. What happens in this instance will be the basis, in the woman's mind and the minds of others, for handling similar correction. He should also take into consideration company precedents regarding similar situations. Chances are she will not accept the supervisor's departing too far from normal procedures.

Help her to find a way to change. This is perhaps the most important part of the correction interview. (Refer to the chapter on appraisal and job performance improvement for guides in developing a program to make the correction.) It should involve changes she thinks she is capable of making. It must include a timetable, specific changes, and a clear outline of how the job must be performed before it can be considered satisfactory. It is often advisable to first put this in writing and then ask for the woman's agreement that the plan is reasonable and attainable.

Make sure that she has an understanding of exactly what is to be done. Ask her to repeat her understanding of the correction that needs to be made and the program that will achieve it. The key to eventual correction and her accountability for making it depends on how well she understands it.

Close the interview pleasantly and make certain that her confidence has not been undermined. The purpose of the interview is to bring about an improvement in job performance. This will not be achieved if she is resentful, confused, or not confident. The supervisor should express his confidence in her job performance and in her ability to make the correction. When she leaves, she should feel secure in her job and should be grateful to the supervisor for having given her the opportunity to improve her chances for success.

Appropriate Follow-up

During the interview, supervisor and subordinate should decide what date they would aim for in having the correction made. Periodic checks can prevent additional errors and keep her on the right track.

If the woman makes an acceptable correction, the supervisor should compliment her and thank her for her cooperation. He should again express confidence in her ability to do the job correctly. This follow-up indicates that the supervisor has noted the correction and that he appreciates the effort involved, but he should not give her the impression that she is being constantly watched. However, if the correction has not been made, a second, possibly firmer, interview should follow.

Correction Spin-off

The supervisor, like the parent or teacher, is constantly faced with the question of deciding on the kind and degree of correction to be made. The use of correction in each instance has far-reaching implications, because the supervisor is, in essence, correcting every woman in his department. When one woman fails to meet the standards of the job, the action he takes represents the policy of the company as far as the other employees are concerned. Each worker considers the supervisor's corrective action is an indication of:

What constitutes a failure to meet job standards.
Whether the policy means what it says.
The company's attitude and reaction toward those who fail to meet job standards.
The supervisor's ability to handle problems associated with incorrect job activity.

What will happen to other employees if they violate the same policy.

The company's fairness in dealing with its workers as related to job performance and adherence to company policy.

The Proper Use of Correction

Correction, like every other leadership activity, is most effective if done at the right time, in the right place, and with the right approach.

Do not have correction interviews too frequently. If used too often, they become a form of nagging and lose their effectiveness. Most minor incidents and job deviations should be handled in the daily interaction between the supervisor and employee. Only the more serious incidents need take the form of correction interviews. Two incidents of lateness might require no more than making the woman aware, in general conversation, that she should try to be more prompt. Don't make too much of it if it is only of minor consequence. However, if her failure to follow company procedures has resulted in a serious mixup in balancing the books, a full correction interview is in order.

Relate the correction to self-interest and job security. If the employee is expected to make a change, show her how she will benefit. (The benefit might be that of retaining her job.) Explain how the correction will be to her advantage, and give her reasons why it should be made.

Be firm when necessary. She will respect firmness if it is fair. Faulty work habits or performance must be corrected, and, if firmness is necessary, use it. The secret is to use the right amounts of softness and firmness in order to achieve maximum effectiveness.

Management has certain rights in establishing work rules and in stating specifically what is considered satisfactory and unsatisfactory job activity. It is easier to correct an employee than to dismiss her. Dismissal often indicates supervisory failure—failure to teach, motivate, or correct appropriately.

Coping with Emotional Reactions to Correction

Every supervisor who works with large numbers of women might occasionally be confronted with a woman who responds to correction with tears. Tears are important in that they give the supervisor insight into sensitive or problem areas. He should acknowledge the tears but continue the conversation. He might shift to a more positive or softer approach or remind her of her strong points and her value to the department. If she seems embarrassed, he should excuse himself for a few minutes and give her a chance to regain her composure. He must bear in mind that she might be the kind of person who would go so far as to cry in a deliberate attempt to unnerve him, so he must keep sight of the purpose of the interview and continue as planned.

There are situations where a supervisor will be well advised to have a third person present when discussing certain areas with women. In fact, some companies require it. Otherwise, it is possible that the supervisor may be misquoted to his or the company's embarrassment. This could even involve lawsuits for improper language or mistreatment. Having a third person present is not recommended under normal circumstances, but only where special problems are anticipated because of the reputation of the woman or the seriousness of the situation.

Promoting Acceptable Standards

The best way to handle correction is to prevent problems from ever arising. It is easier to prevent failures than it is to correct them. Preventing problems is less time-consuming, less of an emotional strain, less uncertain, and encourages efficient performance. The supervisor should engage in daily interaction with all the people in his department to keep standards from falling and to insure adherence to company policies. This means, basically, that a good supervisor engages in effective human relations and is efficient in his job. He is then fulfilling all his responsibilities: training, communicating, motivating, counseling, and providing positive leadership that elicits satisfactory job performance according to the company's standards.

13

The Art
of Counseling Women

EVERY supervisor must act as a counselor—not because he is qualified to or because he wants to, but because his physical proximity and organizational relationship to his subordinates demand it of him. There are marriage counselors, consumer counselors, beauty counselors, financial counselors, and an endless variety of others. Most of them have special training, specific qualifications, and licenses. But the supervisor, who often has little or no special training and is in an unfavorable position to be a counselor because of his position of authority, is forced into counseling women on the job. Counseling often involves problems that are not related to the job, but that still have an effect on the woman and her job performance. She often hesitates to discuss such matters with her immediate supervisor for fear that they will cause him to lower his opinion of her, weaken her promotional opportunities, or possibly affect her day-to-day working relationship with him.

Special Aspects of Counseling Women

At one extreme, some women might be greatly reluctant to discuss personal problems with their male or female supervisors, while others feel compelled to use their supervisors as a sounding board, wanting to discuss *all* problems, even minor ones. They often see the male supervisor as a father figure and feel that their personal problems can be unloaded on him.

Counseling often involves a male-female relationship and problems that might prove embarrassing to both supervisor and subordinate. It might involve a delicate, personal situation that a husband would seriously resent having his wife discuss with another man. A company nurse is most useful for counseling in such areas. She is in a better position to ask probing questions, and women are often more willing to be frank with her.

If a supervisor allows his personal feelings to influence his judgment or if he gives too much advice, he is often considered a meddler. If he listens to all problems, he might find that too much of his time is being consumed. He should remember that his principal role is that of supervising work and employee performance, not operating a private advice bureau. Yet he must recognize the genuine need for counseling his subordinates and handle this responsibility in a way that eliminates interference with job performance.

A wife may complain about her husband and seek the advice of the supervisor as to whether she should leave him. The supervisor can sympathize, but should be cautious in giving advice. A middle-aged woman asked to see her supervisor one day, and opened the conversation with, "Well, he's still at it." The supervisor knew from past experience that this meant her husband was still drinking, wasting his salary, and not supporting her and their three children. "It's getting worse now. He's not mistreating me, but now that the girls are older, he's beginning to embarrass them in front of all their friends." She hesitated for a few moments and then asked, "Don't you think that I have put up with him long enough? Don't you think that I should leave him? Don't you honestly feel that the girls and I would be better off if he were not around?" The supervisor replied, "Mrs. Hilton, you will have to make that decision. You see, I can't possibly know all the circumstances or the effects of what you propose on you, your daughters, or your husband. It wouldn't be fair for me to influence your decision. May I suggest that you talk once again with your minister, and I will be happy to help you get an appointment with a family and children's counseling service if you would like to talk with them."

There is no other way to handle a situation like this. No supervisor has the right to play God with the lives of employees, who must accept the responsibility for their own personal lives. The supervisor is misusing the purpose of counseling if he dispenses personal advice to his employees.

Purpose of Counseling

The purpose of counseling is to minimize or eliminate problems that can or do interfere with morale, productivity, or the harmony of the group. It is a private forum in which the woman has an opportunity to talk to an attentive listener, which may possibly help her to reach an understanding of and solution to her problem. The supervisor does not solve the problem himself nor does he make decisions for her; he merely serves as a sounding board that may help the woman solve her problem herself.

The supervisor's benefit in counseling is that it leads to the solution of a problem that may be interfering with his employee's job performance. By providing a sympathetic ear as well as suggestions, the supervisor may be credited with solving the problem, thus garnering the respect and gratitude of his subordinate. Because counseling can have a strong effect on supervisor-subordinate relations and on the overall efficiency of a department, it should be approached with care through the following channels:

Communication. Inadequate communication or inaccurate information can create problems and build barriers between supervisors and their employees. Counseling provides the opportunity to discover areas of doubt or misunderstanding. The opportunity to talk with her supervisor can often eliminate the anxieties a woman has concerning her progress or job security.

Release of emotional tensions. If a nagging problem is bottled up for too long, it can destroy a woman's peace of mind and eventually result in irritability and decreased productivity. The mere act of talking about such a problem with a sympathetic listener provides partial release from pent-up tensions, even if no solution to the problem has been found.

Mutual reorientation. A woman might be disturbed because she feels a sense of failure in the job. She might be feeling sorry for herself because she didn't get a raise or promotion. Counseling provides the supervisor with the opportunity to know how she feels, and he may find it necessary to reorient his thinking to better cope with this particular employee. He must also try to reorient her thinking so that she has more confidence in her own abilities.

Guidance. The supervisor has a better overall view than his employees of the company's needs. If an employee is concerned about her progress and about her future with the company, the supervisor can provide guidance regarding what she can do to make the progress she wants. If her problems are family-related, he might provide guidance by referring her to a minister, doctor, or the appropriate community service.

Reassurance. Many emotional problems arise from a sense of insecurity and uncertainty. It is generally the fear of what might be, the anxiety created by rumors, or simply a lack of reliable information that causes at least half of job-related anxiety. In many instances, there might be no truth to the rumor, or only some truth. Through counseling the supervisor has a chance to discuss the rumor and eliminate tension or uncertainty.

Employee problem solving. Certain problems must be solved by the individual employee. It would be inappropriate and unwise for the supervisor to impose a decision on her. By providing the opportunity to discuss the problem, think about it, and consider its possible solutions, a supervisor can help the woman discover a satisfactory course of action. The supervisor's most significant role is encouraging the employee to solve her problem herself.

Evidence of the Need for Counseling

When is there a need for counseling? It often arises when there is a sudden change in a woman's job performance or in her relationships with her co-workers. This often indicates that she is wrestling with a problem for which she can find no solution. Certain clues are evidence of a need for counseling: a change in her mood or her approach to her work; her job performance, which has been satisfactory for some time and suddenly becomes unsatisfactory; she is tired most of the time and seems to have no energy; she is involved in a rash of accidents; she makes more than the usual number of careless mistakes; she becomes irritable and resents suggestions, corrections, and all forms of supervision; she becomes a troublemaker; and she is absent or late too often, and obviously doesn't have her mind on her job.

Mrs. Simpson had worked for ten years in the accounting department and was considered an outstanding worker. But over a period of about a month, she seemed to lose interest in her work. She was less dependable and the work of the entire department was seriously affected. During a supervisor-initiated counseling interview, she reluctantly revealed that her husband and two children had been sick. She hadn't told anyone because she considered it a personal problem. As a result of the interview, her supervisor gave her a few days of sick leave. Her family recovered, she got some needed rest, and the company retained a very valuable employee.

The symptoms of problems or disturbances are difficult to discover since many are not job-related. The supervisor's most reliable aid is to know his employees thoroughly and their patterns of work so well that he is able to determine when changes occur.

Initiating the Counseling Session

When a problem arises, either the supervisor or the employee can ask for an interview. The supervisor takes the initiative when he suspects that a change in the job-related activity of the woman is the result of some problem. In initiating the interview, he gives her an opportunity to talk about it and may be instrumental in eliminating the problem completely.

The employee might also ask for an interview and reveal problems of which the supervisor might be unaware.

Harriet Frazier, who worked in the advertising department of a large firm, asked to talk with the personnel director. She revealed that her teen-aged daughter was "running around with the wrong crowd" and that, if she kept it up, it would be just a matter of time before she got into trouble. Mrs. Frazier's only solution seemed to be to stop working, but she wasn't certain whether this would help at all. During the interview, she suddenly thought of a neighbor who might be willing to look after her daughter each day after school. This turned out to be a very satisfactory answer to her problem, one that came about through simple discussion.

Counseling Problems

Counseling problems are usually of a personal nature, whereas correction problems are normally related to job performance. There are an endless variety of personal problems, but many fall into one of the following categories:

Health problems. People cannot be cheerful and enthusiastic about their jobs if they are worried about their health or about the health of their families. If a woman expresses a concern for her health, the supervisor should advise her to seek medical attention, help her in selecting a doctor, and urge her to make an appointment. In many cases, the problems are not serious, and corrective action restores good health and normal job performance.

Financial difficulties. Women seem to be closer than men are to money matters like family finances: buying groceries and children's clothes and paying medical bills. Concern over money or the inability to meet the family's financial obligations keep women in an unsettled state. The supervisor can help by encouraging her to strive for a promotion which will be accompanied by a raise, by providing suggestions concerning family financial guidance, and by informing her of any financial assistance available through the company.

Family problems. These problems are often the most difficult to solve since they are usually emotional and are in areas where the supervisor has almost no influence. If the woman feels that she cannot talk with anyone in her family about the problem, or if she has exhausted her outside resources, the opportunity to talk with her supervisor may, if nothing else, make her feel a little less lonely and the problem seem less burdensome.

Some problems, which are not necessarily personal, are not appropriate for a correction or a joint venture interview. These are best handled in a counseling interview. For example, personality conflicts, jealousy, resentment of authority, conflicts of job interest, and disappointments can decrease productive effort. When co-workers seem to resent a new employee, don't accept her or work cooperatively with her, it is a safe bet that she will become an unhappy and inefficient employee. Counseling interviews with either the co-workers or the new employee are more likely to resolve these problems than any other technique.

Another job-related problem best dealt with in counseling might arise when a woman feels that she is not being paid enough or that her work is not satisfying. During an exit interview, a woman stated that she was resigning because she just wasn't earning enough to make ends meet, and didn't see much hope for a satisfactory increase in pay on her present job. She didn't have another job; she hadn't considered the possibility that it might take some time to find another one, or that the next job at the same skill level might pay the same wages. Nor had she thought much about her loss of employee benefits. She finally agreed that she would be better off not to resign, and her supervisor was eventually able to work with her so that she became eligible for a raise.

Conducting the Counseling Interview

The corrective interview is usually initiated and always controlled by the supervisor. But in counseling interviews, the employee often selects the subject to be discussed, determines what will be said, and guides the direction of the interview. Uniquely, supervisor and subordinate have equal status during counseling, whereas in most other job situations, a distinct supervisor-subordinate status exists.

Since the purpose of the interview is to provide an opportunity for the employee to talk and get a better feel for her problem, the supervisor must make an effort to create the emotional climate conducive to openness and honesty. After all, her willingness to talk is directly related to his willingness to listen. It is the supervisor's responsibility to listen, make helpful comments, and provide suggestions for her consideration. It is not his responsibility to impose his decisions or solutions on her. It is the employee's responsibility to solve her own problem, and in the course of the interview, she might need to be reminded of this fact.

Many supervisors do not have the ideal temperament and patience required for effective counseling. They want to get at solutions too quickly, which does not fulfill the most important function of counseling — providing an interested and sympathetic listener. The counseling interview must be conducted in private. No one should be expected to discuss personal problems in the presence of others. Since the woman is likely to be in a state of emotional anxiety, the supervisor must exert considerable effort to put her at ease, encourage her to talk, and provide opportunities for her to state what's on her mind.

He should not argue or disagree with her. This will make her reluctant to talk about something painful. The supervisor should avoid showing surprise or amazement; he should not be critical. If the employee feels that she has shocked the supervisor, she's likely to back away from further discussion.

The supervisor must communicate a feeling of interest and understanding, and convince her that he is interested in her as an individual. As her trust and confidence in him increase, she will become even more willing to talk. He shouldn't put words in her mouth; let her fumble for them if she must. And he shouldn't try to force conversation about something that she finds too painful to discuss. Given time and encouragement, she will come around at her own pace. He must try to understand those things she avoids bringing to the surface and be able to keep the conversation headed in a direction that will lead to a frank and full discussion of the problem.

Although the supervisor should not provide solutions to problems, he can make a substantial contribution toward their solution by making certain resources available to the employee involved. These might include: (1) promotion and compensation policies of the company that provide realistic career opportunities; (2) employee benefits (including financial assistance); (3) specialized company professional counselors, medical facilities, and personnel, and other available services that might relate to the problem; (4) community services such as religious, governmental, civic, charitable, or other counseling groups that offer assistance.

If the woman sees that she could benefit from one of these four resources, but is reluctant to take the initial step, the supervisor might offer to make arrangements for the first contact.

The supervisor must always remember that the employee has a choice about whether she wants counseling. She doesn't have to talk about personal problems if she chooses not to. Many women resign or are discharged without ever revealing their problems. The woman chooses to engage in the counseling interview and the counseling is effective only if she has confidence in the integrity and ability of her supervisor. Her willingness to talk about her personal problems is the greatest compliment she can pay him. This understanding and respect is an absolute necessity if counseling is to be effective. This respect and understanding are built from daily interaction and *mutual* regard.

It is during counseling that the supervisor comes into his most intimate contact with the women in his department. If he handles the situation skillfully — by listening carefully, by helping her see the nature of the problem more clearly, by suggesting possible solutions she might want to consider, and by calling her attention to available assistance — he will have rendered a most valuable human service. In doing so, he will also earn her eternal gratitude. Effective counseling is a more difficult responsibility than it might seem on the surface. If a supervisor does it well, he will be making a sizable contribution to the goals of the department and the needs of his subordinates. If he doesn't handle it well, he is likely to aggravate the problem, lose the confidence of the employee, and lower the overall productivity of his department.

14

Managing Uniquely
Female Challenges

DO women have more job-related problems than men? If so, what effects do these problems have on their work activities and the leadership of the department?

There seems to be a widespread feeling, at least among supervisors, that women represent more potential problems than men. In a survey by the National Office Management Association, the question was asked, "From your experience, do you find that there are more problem workers among female workers than among men?" Seventy-five percent answered "yes."

Although there are laws against discriminating hiring practices, it is doubtful that all people in a position to hire are free of either conscious or unconscious prejudices against women. There are five common stereotyped ideas that men have about women in the workforce, and so before declining to employ or give women a fair opportunity, all men should ask themselves whether they uphold the beliefs that

Women are absent more often than men.
Women tend to be transient workers.
Women are not ambitious.
Women are more emotional than men.
Women are not suited to men's jobs.[1]

[1] Henry G. Pearson, "Women: Are We Discriminating About Them or Against

Some of these attitudes, beliefs, and so-called common knowledge are subject to considerable differences of opinion and, in some instances, are completely wrong. However, there is occasionally sufficient validity to the claims made about the problems of women workers to require special supervisory attention in areas such as absenteeism, length of employment, limited mobility, influences of age, emotional control, little concern for the job, and a variety of others. This chapter identifies some of these potential problem areas and suggests ways to minimize their interference with work.

Short Length of Employment and High Turnover

The following statistics concern the length of employment and turnover rate of women:
- A study by the U.S. Civil Service Commission revealed that women have a separation rate two and one-half times that of men and that the length of time on the job is three years for women, as compared with five to seven years for men.
- A Labor Department survey regarding women in government indicated that women establish work periods of four-year duration and that women under 30 are prone to quit in one year.[2]

Most surveys and statistics reveal that women have shorter terms of employment and a greater turnover rate than men. After all, it is the woman who leaves her job for childbearing, child rearing, and caring for relatives. It is the woman who resigns when her husband is transferred, when he decides he doesn't want her to work, or when he doesn't like the place or circumstances in which she is working.

As indicated in a previous chapter, more than half the women in the labor force can resign without causing great hardship on themselves or their families' standard of living, whereas men are expected to remain in the labor force until retirement. A woman might not have to enter the labor force at all. But if she does, it is often for a limited time, and she usually can quit whenever she chooses.

The higher rate of female turnover becomes more significant when the cost of turnover is considered. Professor Sumner Slichter, of the Harvard School of Business Administration, gives this breakdown on the cost of turnover in a large industrial firm: [3]

Them?" *Personnel Management—Policies and Practices* (Englewood Cliffs, N.J.: Prentice-Hall, Inc., 1968), p. 249.

[2] *1965 Handbook on Women Workers,* U.S. Department of Labor, 1965.

[3] Edgar S. Ellman, *Managing Women in Business* (Waterford, Conn.: National Foreman's Institute, 1967), p. 26.

Common laborer	$ 126
Semiskilled worker	$ 557
Skilled worker	$18,778

Since statistics indicate a higher turnover rate for women than men and since turnover costs are so high, companies have exhibited increasing concern with finding ways to decrease turnover. Studies indicate that turnover which occurs during the first three months of employment is often the result of improper placement, orientation, or training. Although there are many factors influencing turnover over which the company has no control, a substantial number of "quits" are company caused. The guides in Chapters 4, 5, and 6, if followed, should significantly reduce high turnover.

Dealing with Absenteeism

In a survey involving equal numbers of male and female executives only 25 percent agreed that the absenteeism of women should have any effect on their employment and placement. Professor Herman V. Lamark of Northwestern University has indicated that women have an absentee rate twice that of men and that they are not very concerned with their attendance unless they are the sole breadwinner. Women can stay out for a day with the excuse that they are simply not feeling well. Higher absentee rates exist among women who are unhappy; if they have few friends, if their work group hasn't accepted them, or if they are forced to work for financial reasons. Absenteeism is lower in women over 40 years of age and lowest in women over 50.[4]

One of the difficulties the supervisor must face is that much of a woman's absenteeism is no fault of the company or of the woman. Her absenteeism may result from problems at home. It is she who takes care of family emergencies, children's illnesses, household repairs, and visits to school. The company will seldom take precedence over motherhood and home responsibilities.

A U.S. Department of Labor study indicated the following causes of female absenteeism:

Personal causes

Illness of self or member of family.
Accident involving self or member of family.
Household duties.
Child care.

[4] Herman V. Lamark, "Women in Government" (Chicago: Northwestern University, The Bureau of Business and Industrial Training), p. 168.

Employer causes

Poor selection and placement procedures.
Excessive overwork.
Unpleasant working conditions.
Irregular flow of production.
Ineffective use of skills.
Poor supervision.
Inadequate training or promotion programs.
Ineffective grievance procedures.
Negative employer-employee relations.

Community causes

Inadequate housing.
Lack of convenient shopping facilities.
Poor transportation.
Lack of home services, such as laundry facilities.
Inconvenient banking hours.
Lack of child-care facilities.

Although many female absences are justified, this doesn't mean that the company must stand by and do nothing about the situation. When faced with the problem, management should make an analysis of the number of absences and the days of the week involved to discover prevailing patterns. Further investigation may unearth the real reasons for the absences. The next step is to answer this question, "How seriously is the work affected by the absences, and what are the prospects for correction?" Unfortunately, the following situation arises when there is no other course of action for the personnel manager to take:

"Mrs. Howard, your job performance is excellent. We've always been pleased with your loyalty and high productivity. As a matter of fact, I know that your supervisor considers you one of his very best people. However, you are on an important job that really requires someone to be there every day. I know that we all have to be out once in a while, but you have averaged one day a week for the past several months. I know that your mother-in-law lives with you and when she is ill or when the maid doesn't show up, you must stay home. We already gave you a two-month leave of absence, and you have taken all your vacation for the year. We've talked about this several times, and you've been very honest in stating that you couldn't anticipate any improvement in your absenteeism.

"Although we have been pleased with your work, we simply can't justify keeping you on your present job. When you don't come in, the work of several other people is adversely affected for the day. It's not fair to them or to the company. We certainly appreciate the excellent work you have done. If you become available for work again in the future and feel that you can be more regular in attendance, we will make every effort to give you the same or a comparable job. Your work has been outstanding and certainly makes you eligible to be rehired."

The following is a checklist for preventing and reducing female absenteeism:

> Before employment, determine whether satisfactory arrangements have been made for the care of children and other members of the family living in the home.
>
> Determine whether dependable and satisfactory transportation is available.
>
> In checking references, investigate attendance records and reasons for absenteeism in former jobs.
>
> Check to find out whether there are health problems that might prevent regular attendance.
>
> Inquire into the woman's attitude toward the company, work, and supervision. Find out whether she has to work. Try to determine how well she has gotten along with people in groups before.
>
> Make every effort to place her in the most appropriate job; minimize fatigue and boredom; encourage her acceptance by other members of the group; provide the kind of supervision she wants and needs; make her feel that she is an important member of the team. Let her know that when she is out, she will be missed, and that the work of others will be adversely affected.
>
> Follow up absences. Let her know that you are aware of the absence and that her attendance is important. If she has problems causing the absences, offer to help her when appropriate.

The supervisor must be fair and sympathetic but firm in dealing with excessive absenteeism. Company doctors have estimated that about 50 percent of absences are not absolutely necessary. If the woman has a negative attitude toward the company, the supervisor, and the work, a slight headache might be reason enough for her to decide to stay home. Women who do this are, of course, shortchanging both their own opportunities and those of other women.

The Influence of Age

The greatest instability of women employees is found in the 18 to 20 age group and among women of childbearing age. Maximum stability is reached after the age of 40. In a survey by Edgar S. Ellman, 45 percent of the executives responding stated that women over the age of 45 are likely to be better employees than younger women.[5]

In a National Office Management Association survey, 64 percent of the responding companies indicated that they hire women who are 35 or older for office positions because (1) they are more stable and dependable than younger women; (2) their work is equal to or better than that of younger women; (3) there is less turnover among older women; and (4) a shorter training period is required for older women.

Many older women join the labor force because they are widowed, divorced, or separated, and must often support themselves. Also, it is rare that an older woman will have as many family obligations as a younger woman.

A woman over 40, in reasonably good health, alone or a member of an established family group, has proved to be the most stable female employee. She is less likely to leave, will be absent less often, will respond to company leadership, and will be the best human resource the company can find. However, most companies, because they want to bring young blood into the organization, employ younger women in spite of the statistical evidence that they have a higher turnover, more absenteeism, and more difficult supervisory problems than older women.

Emotional Orientation and Reaction

Women are not necessarily more emotional than men; they simply show their emotions more readily. A man might report a grievance in anger or vent his frustration in other ways. A woman might feel the same way, but react differently. Roberta J. Berkel, the first woman bank manager of the Chemical Bank of New York, remarked, "Women's moods vary more widely and rapidly than men's. I know this from the way my own disposition can vary from day to day, and I take it into consideration in dealing with my female subordinates. Often, a women doesn't know herself why she feels a certain way, and a mood can pass as rapidly as it came on." [6]

Male supervisors have to learn that there are right times and wrong times to correct, praise, and discuss certain subjects with women. At certain times, correction may be gracefully accepted. At other times, the same criticism may result in a thunderous emotional reaction.

[5] Ellman, op. cit.
[6] "Is It Harder to Supervise Women than Men?" *Office Supervisor's Bulletin* (Waterford, Conn.: The Bureau of Business Practice, No. 313, January 30, 1969), p. 5.

As pointed out in previous chapters, women have an emotional orientation to job-related activities and experiences. This does not make them unsatisfactory employees; it can often make them better ones, provided that the supervisor is selective in the timing of his various supervisory contacts with them. And he shouldn't forget that a woman's moods, emotional levels, and reactions can change very quickly.

Little Concern for the Job

His job is often the center of interest for a man, whereas the home is the center of interest for a woman. If she sees most women working in low-paying clerical jobs, she probably reacts with, "Why try?" Many women are not as dependent on their jobs as men to get what they want out of life. And working has not been part of a woman's traditional role. Since she is often not given the opportunity for job growth equal to a man's, she might not have the same intensity of job interest.

This lesser concern for the job often becomes the cause of resignations, lack of interest, absenteeism, and lack of ambition. When a supervisor recognizes this fact, he should make every effort to increase the woman's concern for the job by reminding her of the benefits she can derive from it.

Are Women Too Talkative?

Do women talk more than men? All people like to talk about what interests them. They like to share their common experiences, and women's many roles provide them with areas for conversation men do not have. A woman who is responsible for keeping a house, rearing children, buying groceries, and cooking meals can identify with her co-workers who share the same responsibilities. Thus women have more small talk than men, and the relationships they develop on the job can become more than just working relationships.

In one company a secretary's desk was located in a position out of conversation range with others in the office. The turnover in that position was high until the desk was moved close enough to make conversation possible with the other people in the area.

Women want to talk, and they generally do. Their attachment to the work group and the company will be strengthened if conversation is not prohibited, so long as it does not harm productivity or job performance.

Personal and Outside Problems

Personal and home problems are more serious to women than to men and have more effect on their work. Some women bring their problems to work with them, talk with their co-workers about them, and often seek the sympathy of the supervisor.

The supervisor can be of some assistance in solving problems by following prescribed counseling procedures: by listening, by being patient, and by being available. But some women are burdened with too many problems to be satisfactory employees. The supervisor has to exercise firmness in insisting that job requirements be met; but he should attempt to prevent the problems from jeopardizing her job security. All reasonable corrective steps should be taken before a woman is discharged.

Coping with Her Personal Relationships

Although most women develop good relationships with their co-workers, some are jealous, suspicious, and competitive, which results in personality conflicts. For example, a woman may feel that her home or job is threatened by another woman. She may become suspicious and distrustful of all other women, and carry that feeling over into the work situation. Such a woman can disrupt an entire department. However, the supervisor can minimize conflict and encourage harmonious personal relationships by making all communications clear and complete so that confusion or misunderstandings are avoided; by having firm but flexible rules and practices that provide a secure and structured framework; by not showing favoritism and by insisting on all members of the department meeting standard job requirements; by organizing work assignments efficiently so that lines of authority and responsibility are clear; by being prepared to nip potential conflicts in the bud; and by maintaining relaxed but firm discipline that preserves order, respect, and fairness.

Managing Identifiable Female Types

It is precarious, at best, to relegate women to certain molds or types. However, their special interests and attitudes toward their work and toward other people create sufficient prototypes to justify such considerations.

Mature married women constitute the largest and most important single category of working women from the standpoint of numbers and production. A mature married woman's tenure might be uncertain because of her home obligations; but as long as she is on the job, she will exhibit a strong sense of responsiblity and mature judgment. She will be less flighty and more stable than younger women.

When a supervisor distributes work assignments, he should avoid giving her unscheduled overtime if possible — she probably has a family waiting. The mature married woman can be one of the most profitable producers on the job, but the supervisor must keep her dual role in mind as well as her occasional need to be absent for personal reasons, her uncertain length of employment, and her fixed time schedule. Let her do her best — it will frequently be outstanding.

The dedicated career-minded woman has already proved herself and has achieved some success. She is not usually in low-level positions; her ambition, self-confidence, and abilities have enabled her to obtain a position of responsibility. She tends to be independent, industrious, and both capable of and willing to compete with men. Such a woman can be a tremendously productive asset to the company.

The supervisor of the career woman should give her plenty of goals to work toward. The correction of this type of woman should be soft pressure, not a sharp or stinging rebuke. All that might be necessary is for the supervisor to point her in the right direction, without being critical.

Many career women can be successful, effective, and highly productive members of the workforce without creating any problems. Sometimes, however, an ambitious woman can be difficult to work with and supervise. She might resent criticism of any kind, never admit that she made a mistake, and tend to be overly aggressive in her dealings with other people. Her job and success seem to become more important to her than the niceties of accommodating her co-workers. This woman requires limited but firm leadership if her potential is to be realized.

Younger women may be teenagers fresh out of high school or they may be just recently married. The chief problem with the young woman is that she is immature in her behavior and judgment. In most cases, it is her first job, and she needs some patient understanding and direction while she is trying to settle down. She is usually responsive to supervision since she is accustomed to the authority of her parents and teachers.

Her first few days and weeks on the job are extremely important because it is during this time that she will form lasting work habits. She can be an ideal trainee if she has a quick mind and wants to learn, although she might have difficulty understanding the ways of business and the disciplines required in the work environment. Her supervisor must be firm and relatively uncompromising with her. She can be a star on the team, or one of the chief headaches. It all depends on the kind of guidance she received from her parents and the quality of leadership she gets on her first job.

The marriage hopeful can be a young woman or an older, more mature woman. (A third type might be the single woman who prefers a career to marriage. These are usually interested in their work and will do a good job.) But her age does not really matter. The marriage hopeful views her work as secondary in importance. It is extremely difficult for a supervisor to find a way to motivate a woman to do a good job when she is more interested in getting married. She isn't looking for promotions and is not greatly concerned about pay increases. She is probably far more concerned with how she looks and whether she will be seen at the right places by the right people.

The best bet is to give her a sense of purpose on the job and appeal to her pride. She should want a good recommendation when she leaves, and certainly doesn't want a record of failure. If all else fails, the supervisor must discipline her. He should be firm with her before she loses all interest in her work and adversely influences other members of the department. She can be a disruptive influence and must occasionally be reminded of her real purpose on the job.

There is a serious danger in trying to stereotype people, but these broad generalizations can be useful as general guides. The differences are ones of degree, and lines cannot be so clearly drawn when you move from generalities to real people. A married woman might be immature, and the altar-bound girl might be a steady and responsible worker.

It is especially important not to generalize about women. Although statistics may reveal certain characteristics about the "typical" woman, no one is really typical. Some women might have long terms of service, few absences, and a minimum of problems.

However, if a supervisor has problems with his female subordinates, he can use the problems as stepping-stones for developing desirable characteristics and increasing production. If his awareness of potential problem areas makes him cautious in selecting, placing, and working with women, his extra care will serve to build the kind of workforce that has the greatest performance potential. His success will depend on his effectiveness in preventing problems from developing and on his skill in coping with those that do develop. As in other areas of supervision, the wisest course of action is to maintain a climate that will minimize problems and maximize productivity. In spite of potential problem areas, women make outstanding employees, and many of them create no more problems than do men.

part four

Her Potential
for Leadership

15

Women's
Leadership Potential

MANY executives who believe that women make satisfactory employees state emphatically that they do not make good supervisors.
However, the facts prove that this is not true. Women can and do make
very successful supervisors and executives. The number of women
entering higher leadership levels is increasing, and women are handling
top executive jobs effectively.

Women possess characteristics and qualifications that give them
unique advantages over men as supervisors; but, paradoxically, these
same ingredients are often the stumbling blocks to their effective
leadership. A woman encounters obstacles to her executive status in
three areas: (1) within herself, (2) the prejudices against her felt by
both sexes at all levels, and (3) within the job requirements and structure of the company.

This chapter analyzes the strengths and weaknesses of women as
they seek to fill leadership positions. Identification of the specific
problems should enable the potential woman executive and the
company to make adjustments that will help her make the leadership
contribution she is capable of making.

The Demands of Leadership

If women are to be effective supervisors and if the company is to
reap the benefits of their contributions, both must be aware of the re-

quirements and demands of leadership roles. It is assumed that the demands will be the same for both sexes, even though many executives think that women have to be superior in their performance in order to reach the same level of achievement. Business leadership usually requires:

Generous amounts of education and experience.

Willingness to work long hours, travel, relocate, and continue personal development.

Objectivity, decisiveness, courage to stand up and be counted, confidence in other people, willingness to delegate, and acceptance of decisions based on achievement.

Acceptance of responsibility and determination to insure that the right things happen.

Willingness to put the job first, to focus on goal-oriented activity, and to avoid personality conflicts or differences.

Ability to accept constructive criticism gracefully and gratefully and to make corrections.

Capacity to develop and maintain effective relationships with supervisors, peers, subordinates, and the public.

Desire to compete and win.

Many women are simply not willing to pay the full price in time and effort demanded of leadership. But leadership success cannot be attained at a discount. One woman executive remarked that women who asked about her work were horrified to learn that she put in 60 to 70 hours a week. Some women just don't want that kind of life, and some don't want the responsibility.

In recent years, the popular style of leadership has shifted from the physically strong, loud, aggressive, and always-in-motion type to one characterized by teaching, persuading, informing, helping, and being sensitive to human needs and reactions. This shift from strength to persuasion is ideal for women because they are adept at persuasion. Women's leadership strength lies in the decisive human areas of patience, understanding, sympathy, counseling, teaching, and graciousness, all of which enhance their suitability for executive responsibility.

Measuring Leadership Potential

Answers to the question "Do women make effective leaders?" are so diverse and in some cases so extreme that it is difficult to believe that people are talking about the same thing. One executive commented, "When the pressures build and the in-fighting becomes intense, emotions take over and the 'tigress' of management reverts to her role of the purring, whimpering kitten who seeks protection of her male master."

At the other extreme is the executive who said, "I have found that women make better managers than men. They are more reliable, take more interest in their work, have less tendency to be away from their jobs, and are more alert and loyal."

Between these two extremes are more moderate opinions and evaluations, and overall experience justifies management's confidence in women as potentially outstanding executives. There is no evidence that women lack analytical ability, aggressiveness, or innovative and scientific imagination. Nor is there any evidence that the end results of research are influenced by the sex of the person doing the research.

In evaluating the potential of a woman for leadership and promotions, management must always remember that the merits of that particular woman are under consideration, not typical statements and statistics about all women. If a woman has the qualifications for a leadership position, she should get the job. If she deserves a promotion, she should be promoted. If a particular woman is not the best qualified applicant, she should not be given the job.

The Number of Women Executives

Trends in the total number of women executives should be very encouraging to women and to companies who need good leadership. However, the percentage of the total number of executive positions occupied by women is relatively static and not as impressive.

The greatest strides have been made in department stores, where 50 percent of the executives are women. The percentage for insurance companies is 25 and for banks, 10. Consider these statistics:

The number of women executives (defined as those earning more than $10,000 a year) tripled — 8,875 to 25,457 — between 1950 and 1960. But during this same period, the number of men at this level increased from 428,350 to 1,156,817. Thus, women remained at about 2 percent of the total. "In essence the absolute number of women executives increased dramatically, but their proportion to male executives in the workforce did not change appreciably." [1]

About 9 percent of working men earn $10,000 a year or more, but less than 1 percent of working women earn that much. [2]

[1] Garda W. Bowman, et al., "Are Women Executives People?" *Harvard Business Review* (July–August, 1965), p. 22.
[2] Ibid.

The higher the position, the less likely it is to be filled by a woman. In 1964 when the Civil Rights Act was passed, women held about 68 percent of the Grade 5 jobs in the federal civil service; but at each grade higher, the proportion of women dwindled.

It is easy to think that women are taking over many executive positions, because every time they achieve positions previously held by men, conversation and publicity result. For example, it was big news when the first woman was accepted as a member of the New York Stock Exchange. Although it's true that women are moving into most higher-level executive positions in greater numbers than ever before, the number of men in these positions has also increased. A woman executive is a highly visible statistic and can delude a company into thinking that it has more women executives than it actually has.

Handicaps Women Encounter on the Way to the Executive Suite

Men who are against women holding management positions usually fall into one of two categories: (1) those who believe that women aren't as good as men; and (2) those who feel threatened by having to compete with women.

Another obstacle to women managers is that most men prefer not to be supervised by women. Also, most women prefer not to be supervised by women. This is the crux of the dilemma women supervisors face. They step into the batter's box with at least one strike against them.

However, this doesn't mean that women shouldn't hold supervisory jobs; it simply indicates a need for very careful selection and training of those who are to become supervisors. And, since women are the second choice, they have to try harder, be more careful to follow the rules of effective leadership, and perhaps conduct their working relationships with more caution than men.

Women managers face even more problems. Once a woman is in a supervisory position, she might have a lot of trouble hiring men and maintaining discipline of her staff. She may be a prime target for criticism from her subordinates, her peers, and her supervisors. So she will have to make fewer mistakes than men in order to hold her own.

All the obstacles that women supervisors face can be boiled down to one overriding problem—prejudice. Caroline Bird said, "The bigger the job, the less likely it's held by a woman. Whether the measure is money, power, prestige, or achievement, and whatever the field, the proportion of women at the top is remarkably constant and low." She cites the "invisible barriers" of male prejudice, traditional male and female jobs, male-oriented company policies and organization, and lack of confidence in women as the "high cost of keeping women down." [3]

Criticism of Women as Supervisors

How much of the criticism of women bosses is really justified? As we attempt to evaluate her qualifications for leadership, these criticisms deserve careful scrutiny so that we can determine to what extent the criticism is valid. Some common criticisms of women are:

They do not give sufficient credit to the people who work with them or for them.

They often feel insecure in their jobs and so they guard against anyone else becoming good enough to threaten their status.

They take things too personally. They do not separate personal loyalty from company loyalty.

They are too fussy, too nosy, and too hard to please. They don't have enough confidence in others to delegate responsibility.

They are too skeptical of other women. They are willing to admit that women are good at putting things over on men, but they are overly suspicious of women trying to put something over on them.

They are not as interesting and exciting as male supervisors.

They are too emotional and sensitive; therefore, they cannot stand the pressures of management or render objective decisions.

Many women dislike working for a woman because they say that men are more thoughtful and fair bosses. Furthermore, if a female subordinate is the kind of woman who makes a habit of using her feminine wiles to get her own way with a male boss, all her efforts will be useless if her supervisor is a woman. This leads to resentment and bitterness.

Much of the criticism leveled at women supervisors is obviously not justified. However, female characteristics such as inquisitiveness, emotional reactions, and the tendency to base decisions on intuition as well as on logic can act as both positive and negative factors in supervisory relationships.

Women supervisors should give themselves all the constructive correction that is warranted. This should include correction in areas

---

[3] Caroline Bird with Sara Welles Briller, *Born Female — The High Cost of Keeping Women Down* (New York: David McKay Company, Inc., 1968).

where they are subject to the most criticism. The company should use its influence to develop programs that seek to confront and minimize unjustified criticism of women as supervisors.

The Influence of Men on Women's Leadership Role

In the final analysis, it is men who now evaluate the leadership potential of women and decide whether women will be given positions of leadership in the company. Thus, if women want to be accepted and promoted as executives, they must convince men that they are just as capable of carrying out executive responsibilities as men.

Unfortunately, some men still consider women problem workers. They believe that women want and expect special privileges. And they believe that women are only temporary employees despite the fact that a woman who is being considered for a supervisory position has already achieved at least a modicum of success in her job and has proved that she takes her career seriously.

It is this kind of entrenched attitude that women encounter and must be prepared to cope with if they are to be effective executives. An unjust attitude does not make the problem any less real. As long as the attitude exists, the obstacle must be hurdled.

Since women can and do fill all types and levels of executive positions with good results, the male-oriented company and women should work cooperatively to evaluate objectively women's potential for leadership.

Women Can Be Outstanding Leaders

All companies should prefer a competent female supervisor to an incompetent male any day of the week. The sad fact is that this is not always the case—incompetent men have been promoted over competent women for years. Results-oriented management that compensates and promotes according to performance is a boon to the opportunities for women. All women ask is a "fair shake" and to be judged by their performance. However, the company whose policies are made by male executives has to change its practices so that it can benefit from the valuable and almost untapped potential of women.

In spite of handicaps and the reluctance of people to work for female supervisors, women perform as first-rate executives. If women believe in themselves, they can be successful executives. Every time a woman displays unreasonable reluctance to work for another woman, she is sabotaging her own opportunities for promotion. Higher management positions will be more available when women exhibit a willingness to accept female supervision.

It is to the everlasting credit of women supervisors that, despite the obstacles they encounter, they are filling management positions at all levels in increasing numbers. They have demonstrated that they can measure up in every respect to the requirements of executive leadership. They are being accepted by subordinates and superiors, and are demonstrating that they can get the job done.

16

Accelerating
Her Upward Mobility

MANY women are interested in promotions and in all forms of upward mobility. And most companies are interested in advancing these women up the management ladder. They have vacancies that must be filled if the company is to advance and grow. If a woman is qualified and has proved her abilities on the job time and time again, everyone — the company, the department, her co-workers, the stockholders, and the public — loses if she is not promoted.

The openings and opportunities are there at all levels and in almost every job category. Whether women will fill their share of these openings depends largely on their availability for career-oriented executive positions, which might involve many years of effort; their willingness to continue their education and development on the job; their success in producing outstanding results in order to deserve promotions; and their ability to motivate themselves and to exhibit maturity in human relations and in judgment.

Woman's share of new openings also depends on the company's success in providing developmental programs and an internal organization suitable to her needs and its ability to insure promotions based on merit.

Women's Excellent Qualifications for Leadership

Women might have limited business experience, but many of them offset this with management experience in the home. They have managed the family finances, solved problems, and made decisions. They have learned to economize, to save time by developing efficient methods, and to maintain harmony. They have served as members of the P.T.A. and the church and have been active in fund raising and other group and public activities. Much of this experience can be transferred to their jobs and to supervisory roles.

Mrs. Estill Buchanan, a management consultant from Boulder, Colorado, states:

> Women are psychologically attuned to the new concept of business team leadership. The emphasis today is on modern decentralized organizations in which power accrues to those individuals who can effectively link groups through competence in communications. The old concept of a boss in absolute command over his area is yielding; that is masculine and outdated.[1]

There is no doubt that women are adequately qualified for positions of business leadership. As a matter of fact, in areas of communications, empathy, human relations, and understanding, they are outstanding. The key to a woman's upward mobility is the effectiveness with which she and the company work together to make the most of her full potential.

Selecting the Right Women for Leadership and Promotion

To be selected for supervisory positions, women need the same qualifications men need—the ability to persuade, to lead, to win respect, to plan analytically, to mold a team, and to work effectively with all types of people. Most companies might give some consideration to a woman's expected length of employment and the demands of her home responsibilities. As in the case of a man, she should be given all possible training in human relations and supervision. She must be given assistance in learning to make quick, accurate decisions based on facts, to handle a variety of problems, and to compliment or correct her subordinates when necessary.

Once a company decides to expend time and effort in promoting a woman or in grooming her for an executive spot, it is investing con-

---

[1] "For Women, a Difficult Climb to the Top," *Business Week* (August 2, 1969).

siderable money in that woman's future contribution. It assumes that a woman intends to stay on the job and that she will exert herself to meet the expectations of the company. Sometimes, of course, the company will lose — if, for example, a college graduate with executive potential decides to give up her career for a home and family. However, there's no sense in assuming that all women will do this just because some do. A woman who wants to move up, who wants responsibility, and who genuinely likes her job is not likely to give it up unless she has no choice.

A woman must be selected because her qualifications best fit the requirements of the position to be filled. After she is selected, every effort should be made to train her in all areas of supervision before she assumes her responsibilities. Hence, she will be able to perform satisfactorily from the outset; she will have confidence in herself, thereby making it easier for her to convince others of her abilities. An older woman often has a better chance of being accepted. Younger ones might have trouble supervising men or older women regardless of their ability.

Development Programs

Most enlightened companies and executives today want to see women advance rapidly in all areas of management, and they are willing to structure supervisory training programs to develop women's leadership skills. Women will increasingly find that company management programs will be open to them and that many of these programs will provide them with special assistance.

Company leadership programs should be structured to prepare women for jobs that they can expect to occupy. The requirements of these jobs must be analyzed — what they will be required to know, skills that they must master, and knowledge they will need to get the job done properly. If women do not have the same mechanical skills, competitive drive, aggressiveness, ambition, analytical reasoning, and decision-making ability as men, special emphasis should be placed on them in company-sponsored training programs.

Management should not only give systematic, thorough attention to qualifying women for first-line supervisory positions but should also have programs and on-the-job training for women at all levels so that they will be prepared to move rapidly into higher managerial positions.

Preparing Herself for Advancement

It is true that leaders are made, not born, and that the most crucial ingredient for success is that supplied by the person involved. Competition for the available supervisory openings demands that people — men or women — motivate themselves to go beyond the minimum requirements of company programs. The people who do are the ones who will excel. If women are to move up in management, personal guidance and company programs should encourage them by giving advice such as this:

> Never stop studying and learning. . . . Look for courses offered in your field and take them. Don't rule out a profession simply because it is predominantly male. . . . Set your sights high. Don't defeat yourself at the outset by assuming that you can't advance because you are a woman.
>
> Don't waste your time and talents working for an organization that doesn't give responsible positions to women. Try not to be conscious of being a "woman in business." You are, of course, but calling attention to the fact only makes your colleagues, women as well as men, uncomfortable. Concentrate on the work.
>
> Yes, you can marry and have children and still pursue a career. But you will have to find a husband who respects your independence rather than resents it.[2]

A woman can, on her own initiative, continue her education and set high standards for herself. Before she can expect to advance, she must first learn to perform one job extremely well, then another and another until she has developed and mastered many skills in different areas. She must set a goal for herself, commit herself to it, and then use all her resources to achieve it. She should not let an unpleasant job or task deter her from what she wants. She can turn a job she dislikes into one she likes and be prepared to cope with all kinds of situations — some of which may be ideal, others not. And in conjunction with hard work and dedication, she must develop the ability to get along with all the people she comes in contact with. Even if she does not work directly with them now, they may prove to be helpful to her later on.

Women at the top have beaten the system by virtue of their ability, their instinct for improvisation, and their exceptionally strong motivation. And women who expect to reach the top must be willing to pay the price.

Disadvantages and Roadblocks to Be Overcome

Traditional attitudes have placed roadblocks in women's path to the executive suite. They can react to these roadblocks by ignoring or

---

[2] "How Good Are Women Bosses?" *Changing Times* (April 1967), p. 17.

resenting them and feeling defensive and negative, or by exerting every effort to overcome them and to succeed in spite of them. The second way is the most sensible and the one most likely to have lasting effects. The following are areas that deserve special attention if women are to move up in business:

The perquisites of rank. Caroline Bird has stated, "Every responsible manager, man or woman, needs support from above and below, access to information, broad experience outside the immediate organization, and the self-confidence to make decisions. Leaders must be recognized as leaders so that others will follow them. . . . All organizations resist giving these perquisites (pay, title, rank, decorated offices, secretarial help, and authoritative information) to a woman. Almost every sizable organization has some women exercising authority on an informal and undefined basis." [3]

Women (or men) cannot qualify for leadership positions, perform effectively in those positions, or prepare adequately for higher positions if they are in a vacuum. They must have authentic, interactive, two-way communication with all individuals and groups whose functions or authority can influence their chances for advancement. If a woman executive is isolated, she is denied the opportunity to move up. In order for her to function as a part of the management team, she must have equal worth and equal weight with the other members of the team. If management really wants her to succeed, it must take positive action to insure that she is given opportunities in all areas.

Cultural conditioning. Our culture tends to veer women away from wanting or qualifying for positions of responsibility in business life. Girls are taught the "feminine" virtues of keeping house and rearing children, discouraged from participating in rough sports, and encouraged to build on and play up their attractiveness to men. Because women have adapted to this cultural "truth" for thousands of years, they (and men) are conditioned to believe that women are less qualified for the rigors of management than men.

It takes overt effort on the part of women and management to effect a change in this conditioning, thinking, and cultural mold. Deliberate initiative should be taken to overcome this leadership lag so that women's potential can be used.

Dedication and commitment. It takes exceptional commitment for a woman to overcome the obstacles she encounters. The fact that many women do not have to work, but want to, suggests that a woman's com-

---

[3] Caroline Bird, "Women in Business: The Invisible Bar," *Personnel* (May–June 1968), p. 34.

mitment to her career may actually be deeper than a man's. She is in her position more as a result of free choice, preference, and desire than men in similar positions, who have to work and are, in some cases, forced to accept their situation because they simply have no choice. Because a woman voluntarily chooses a career in management and remains in it because she likes it, she is more likely to feel stronger dedication and commitment than a man.

But when the chips are down, women are in the minority in management and must face prejudices and policies that still stand in the way of their success. So women must be prepared for a struggle if they are to achieve their goals.

Strength of her ambition. In a study conducted during the 1960s by the U.S. Department of Labor, several hundred women in high-level positions in business and industry were asked what positions they would like to be holding five years hence. Fifteen percent wanted to be retired; 86 percent wanted to keep on working; but only 40 percent hoped to be promoted to better positions. Many women do not try to qualify for better positions. Perhaps it is because of their conditioning, which was discussed earlier, and perhaps because of their reluctance to face the stiff corporate competition, the problems ambitious women often encounter in business, and the fear of losing. If they regard the obstacles most women face in their climb to the top as insurmountable, they will never get anywhere. Therefore, a woman who is ambitious must also be optimistic.

Perhaps there are reasons for a woman to be discouraged, but being discouraged does not necessarily mean giving up. She can succeed if she tempers her ambition with outstanding performance and hard work. A female executive who has made it to the top advised, "Women have to ask for the promotion. Too many women sit in silence and are overlooked because no one knows they want to assume additional responsibilities." A woman must have sufficient ambition to want to advance, to be able to convince others that she is serious about her career, and to be willing to implement this ambition with the action required for upward executive mobility. She must be the best qualified; and she must want a continuously expanding career in management. But the company must provide the stimulus and road maps for her climb.

The Importance of Continuing Education

Perhaps the most significant influence on the opening of promotional opportunities for women is education. This includes company-sponsored as well as outside programs.

Of the thousands of executives who attend management courses, only a very small number are women. There are perhaps several reasons for this: Women now represent only a small percentage of higher management; their companies are reluctant to send them; and women are reluctant to be away from their homes and families for the time required. Some women have expressed the feeling that management courses, in their promotional literature and in their attendance, are traditionally male-oriented and that women feel unwelcome and out of place.

However, education is crucial to a woman's career, so she must make an extra effort to attend courses that will further her career. If a man and a woman are up for the same job and have equal qualifications, the odds are that the man will receive the promotion. A woman who has extra credentials and who has shown initiative and dedication beyond what is normally called for will be more likely to get the job.

The better educated a woman is, the better her chances for career advancement. Most major companies now recruit women on the college campus for technical, professional, and general junior executive training programs. The law requires that women not be discriminated against regarding employment, that they be paid comparable salaries, that they be given equal access to training, and that they be given equal promotional opportunities. Companies, in trying to comply with the law and in attempting to keep their management positions filled, are stepping up their search for the woman with the educational and personal qualifications that can make her a good risk for filling the job that can lead to an executive career.

Increasing Opportunities for Executive Leadership

Women have justified their claim to the executive suite. More than ever before, executive positions of all kinds and at all levels are available to qualified women. The changing requirements of leadership are opening new and more management doors to women. A look at the future's potential need for executives leaves little doubt that women will fill an increasing number of top-level positions. Opportunities for women are multiplying rapidly, particularly with companies that produce, advertise, or sell consumer-oriented products and services. Such companies realize that it serves their best interests to have women executives in decision-making positions when their products and services will eventually be used by women.

It is to the credit of women executives that in spite of adversity they have climbed to the ranks of management at all levels. They have demonstrated that they can measure up in every respect to the requirements of executive leadership. They are being accepted, if not always welcomed, by employees and management and are demonstrating that they know how to get the job done.

Women's upward mobility can be accelerated even faster with an awareness on the part of women that, although most prejudice against them as managers is gone, some still remains. This knowledge should motivate women to work even harder to win the respect and approval of others by doing the job so well that they will merit promotions.

Women should try to be objective in their relationships with people and in their work. An increased sense of security and self-confidence will promote objective thinking. Furthermore, if women expect to be effective supervisors, they had better be prepared to work at it, to continue their educational pursuits, and to be industrious and dedicated in the eyes of their associates. Women still have to convince others they are serious about their careers. Management doesn't want to gamble on the stability of its leadership. Too much is at stake.

A successful executive, whether a man or woman, is formed over an extended period of time, sharpened by experience, stimulated by reward and encouragement, goaded by mistakes, and seasoned by the opportunity to exercise judgment. Even the most competent women will not become good high-level managers if the company denies them the essential room and freedom for growth.

Women can become and are becoming superior managers at all management levels. A woman's upward growth should be viewed as a cooperative effort on the part of the company and the woman herself. Perhaps the most important reminder for management is its responsibility to use its total human resource potential, including the executive ability of women; its legal and moral obligation to give women an equal opportunity for executive growth; and a caution that women should not be evaluated as statistics but as unique individuals in relation to job requirements. If the person qualifies, promote her (or him).

Women have to do their share. Perhaps they have been required to do more than their share. But if a woman wants the rewards of an executive position, she must be willing to go after it. And the path will grow smoother as she continues to justify her executive status.

part five

Trends and Conclusions Regarding Working Women

17

Dynamic
Trends and Changes
Affecting Women

HOW far have women really come in their struggle for equal job opportunity, equal pay, equal status, and equal representation in all areas of the nation's public and business life? Gladys Tillett, U.S. representative to the United Nations Commission on the Status of Women, stated:

> Although the divine right of kings to rule over the masses of men was forever destroyed by the American Revolution, it left untouched the divine right of men to rule over women. Both men and women accepted the divine right of men to rule over women with equal sincerity. The church taught it. The law endorsed it. Men claimed it as the "law of God." . . . The advances made by women in the last century and a half have been significant and dramatic. For example, a little more than 150 years ago there was not a single woman college graduate in the entire world; no woman could collect her own wages. . . . It is an impressive fact that the customs of two-thirds of the women in the world have changed to a greater extent in our lifetime than they had changed in the previous 2000 years.[1]

There can be little doubt that women have indeed made dramatic strides in a comparatively short period of time, but American women

[1] As quoted in the *Charlotte Observer* (October 31, 1968).

will push for an even bigger role in business, and public life — and they will get it. However, it will not come about without adjustments by women, men, business, and society. And these adjustments will not be made without some explosive reactions from both sexes.

The Business World in Transition

Women's world is changing with the recognition that they can combine marriage and motherhood with a lifelong career in which interruptions for childbearing and rearing are reduced to sabbaticals lasting only several years at most.

Women's increased upward mobility is causing tension and anxiety among men as they are forced to compete with women for jobs and management positions. One woman executive states, "So long as rigid division of labor existed, the services of the sexes were not competitive, but complementary. . . . Now there has been a shrinkage of the two extremes, of the heavy jobs that only men could do and the home jobs that only women could do, leaving a constantly widening field of in-between jobs that either sex might do . . . a situation bringing about an ever-increasing competition and tension between the sexes."[2]

People seldom feel comfortable in this kind of unsettled, transitional, changing climate. Yet it is out of this unstable state that women's greatest challenges and opportunities will emerge. Rigidity is breaking down; tradition is giving way; and new forms of organization, thinking, and opportunities are evolving. If women are to move forward, they must take full advantage of the opportunities afforded by these changes. They can, of course, resist change, ignore reality, and lament for the dying past, but it will be to no avail. The tide is turning in women's favor and they must swim with it with a full measure of energy and commitment if they are to fit into a new world.

Almost all indicators of the dynamic changes occurring in management point to the increased upward mobility of women. People in every aspect of management are shifting their attitudes in women's favor from personal judgments to objective and quantitative appraisal. The emphasis is moving toward rewarding and promoting without regard to sex.

Women's Future in the Business World

As a woman's role in the outside world shifts its base, business must view her in a different light. A look at her future place in the

---

[2] Garda W. Bowman, et al., "Are Women Executives People?" *Harvard Business Review* (July–August, 1965), p. 24.

social and economic world provides keys to what she and the employer can expect of her tomorrow.

A woman no longer has to wonder, "What kind of job can I get?" She can now realistically ask herself, "What kind of job do I want?" Women's attitudes toward their jobs and their acceptance by employers are constantly being altered by scientific and technological changes, educational opportunities, men's military requirements, space-age developments, the population boom, changes in cultural attitudes, and the changing age level of women workers. And as women change their attitudes and thinking, their image of themselves, their place in society and business, and their contribution potential, management had better be prepared to meet such changes with new concepts and responses.

An editorial stated:

> Men may find it difficult to contemplate with anything approaching equanimity a world in which women are really equal to them, but it would be a good idea for them at least to make a try. The reason is simple: exactly that state of affairs is certain to be here a lot sooner than most people imagine. Women comprise over half of the country's voting population. . . . It's a bit odd that they have been excluded from the "power structure" or the corporate decision-making machinery. But before they can demand equal participation in urban affairs and business, they must make up for their delinquency by using the brains and education with which they have been endowed.[3]

Womanpower as an Organized Force

The movement for women's liberation has become a force gaining momentum every day. Evelyne Sullerot of France once remarked, "I've seriously considered a revolution, but it wouldn't achieve our purpose. Successful revolutionaries end up in control. But all we are after is equality."[4]

In one respect a revolution is already under way. With recent court decisions and legislation, women's rights are protected by law. Now all the women have to do is take advantage of the rights guaranteed them.

Margaret Mead has stated:

> The few feminist activities today are rebelling against a life style that makes living conditions difficult rather than against legal and eco-

---

[3] *McCall's* (November 1967), p. 4.
[4] As quoted in the *Charlotte Observer* (May 23, 1969).

nomic restrictions. The professions are open to women, and so are
the universities and business. But while there are no closed doors for
them to batter down, there is a style of life that makes it more difficult
for a woman to attain any degree of success in the business world.
The fact that formal barriers are down reduces women to battling with
feather-soft barriers that never really yield, but instead smother the
attacker. . . . They simply live in a society that burdens them with
managerial and maintenance chores.[5]

Many organized groups of women, such as NOW (National Organization for Women) have been formed for the purpose of ending sex
discrimination in hiring, promotions, and salaries; for repealing abor-
tion laws; for establishing comprehensive child-care facilities; and for
placing women in policy-making positions. As with all activist groups,
it is wrong to assume that the most vocal and most radical are thoroughly representative. But there is no escaping the need for recognition of the demands being made.

An article in *Look* magazine refers to women as the next rebels:
the half of our population that is underpaid, barred from major jobs,
and often mocked.

> For many women, a long-suppressed rage is now beginning to surface,
> and their movement for equal rights is becoming organized and gain-
> ing momentum. We are on the brink of another massive rebellion —
> the rebellion of women — one that is bound to have a profound impact
> on all of us and one that could lead to severe disruption, even a major
> upheaval of our society.
>
> It might actually overshadow the black revolution and the student
> protests because it involves not another minority, but this time a
> majority of Americans — 51 percent. . . . When women revolt, all of
> us will change. We will not be able to escape this rebellion because
> it reaches into every institution in our society and affects our most
> personal and intimate relationships. . . . Mothers and wives and
> daughters and teachers and secretaries and girl friends cannot be
> ignored. Paradoxically, it is probably still too early to see the full
> potential for women's rebellion and already too late to avoid it." [6]

Kate Millett has exerted a serious impact on equal rights for women
through her in-depth study [7] of the sexual revolution. She contends that

[5] Margaret Mead, "Women Seek Illusive Dream," *Richmond Times-Dispatch* (November 2, 1969).
[6] Richard E. Farson, "The Rage of Women," *Look* (December 16, 1969), p. 21.
[7] Kate Millett, *Sexual Politics* (New York: Doubleday, 1970).

much of the patriarchal bias of the past continues to operate in modern culture to deny equal rights to women. She uses the works of several modern fiction writers to justify her contention that the whole world of political influence has been condescending and limiting to women.

We have seen only the initial stages of this rebellion by women. Management's attitude must be forward looking enough to anticipate events and to accord recognition to what is a valid political and economic force. In areas such as consumer quality and prices, political candidates, and education, organized women have long had substantial impact. The same pressures are now being directed against employers for job rights and for full recognition.

Protesting and boycotting women have achieved a rollback in grocery prices. The Equal Employment Opportunity Commission has charged a leading manufacturer with discriminating against women in layoffs and discharges. The company has been required to compensate the women for loss of pay and to rehire those discriminated against.

National news services have reported, on numerous occasions, when women have instituted legal action, through private attorneys and government agencies, against present and former employers. They have charged discrimination and failure to employ women for certain jobs or to provide equal pay and promotion opportunities.

The U.S. Supreme Court ruled in 1971 that it was illegal to use tests or other job requirements not proved valid for the specific job for which the applicant is being considered. This decision strikes down the use of tests or other requirements which might not relate specifically and realistically to a woman's qualifications for a particular job.

New Breakthroughs

The U.S. Department of Labor predicts that as the need for increased family income continues and as labor-saving household equipment is improved, more and more women will seek employment outside the home. When this occurs, many management levels and areas of business which have been exclusively male will become open to women. And, once the barrier has been crossed, increasing numbers of women will enter all kinds of positions.

The best bet for mature women returning to work are occupations such as teaching, nursing, retail selling, food service, telephone service, medical service, social work, local government, public relations, real estate, insurance, and market research.

The computer world is a relatively new area, and is wide open for women. They represent 40 percent of the programmers and mathematicians who harness the computers at Bell Laboratories. IBM, which probably employs more women in technical jobs than any other company, scours college campuses for women graduates in mathematics and science. The whole field of computer technology is one of the fastest-growing areas of opportunity for women. In addition, women will soon be able to find jobs in all areas of management and other once "restricted" occupations.

As women plan their education and careers, they should look to the future and what tomorrow's job opportunities are likely to be. They should assume that all areas will be open to them if they are willing to get the education necessary to meet the requirements of the job.

A survey in *U.S. News & World Report* stated:

> Education turns out to be a factor in determining how likely a woman is to seek a job. Regardless of income, a woman who is well educated is more likely to work than one who is not. On the average, 51 percent of married women who are college graduates hold jobs. Only 33 percent of married women who never finished high school are at work.
>
> Almost 64 percent of college-educated women whose husbands earn between $7,000 and $10,000 are working. Only 27 percent of women with less than a high school education and whose husbands earn less than $3,000 are employed.[8]

Women can't fill tomorrow's jobs with yesterday's knowledge and skills. The basis for their achievement in business is their education. If a woman seeks a career as soon as she finishes school or if she expects to enter business after rearing a family, her education will determine at what level she enters and how far she goes.

Formal education is a prerequisite for most of the better technical, professional, skilled, and management jobs. In many college placement offices, women graduates as a matter of routine are getting business positions that would have been closed to them ten years ago. Those with advanced degrees in certain fields often have their pick of the well-paying, prestigious, first-rung jobs.

In addition to formal education, a great variety of other educational opportunities exist. Special correspondence courses are available; local technical and trade schools conduct courses while the children are in school or at night when husbands can baby-sit. Many YWCAs, private business colleges, and local community groups provide endless educational opportunities for women. Most of these courses are avail-

[8] "Rebelling Women—The Reason," *U.S. News & World Report* (April 13, 1970), p. 37.

able at convenient locations and hours, at reasonable fees, and require limited or no educational enrollment requirements.

In this area, everyone agrees that the greatest influence on the future job opportunities of women will be their educational qualifications. But women must respond with the willingness and perseverance necessary to qualify themselves for careers.

Estill Buchanan, in the *Colorado Business Review,* offers the following suggestions to management for creating programs that will develop women's full managerial potential:

1. Open up the entire program for management training and development to women.

• Extend management training programs now geared to recent college graduates to the mature, college-educated women now starting a full-time career.

• Expect the mature woman's training to advance more rapidly and accelerate her progress accordingly.

• Open to qualified women the higher levels of in-service training, within their related job rotation and cross-functional assignments.

• Grant her objective performance evaluation, with straightforward, constructive criticism, without soft-pedaling from fear of imagined sensitivity.

• Expect satisfactory performance and reward it with commensurate pay, promotion, status, and privileges.

• Open the training ladder at more position levels, so that a mature woman with relevant experience may be added in at the most appropriate rung.

• Broaden the training program by including interim jobs that provide equivalent development experiences that are not now seen as part of executive development sequences.

• Rethink distributed experience within the company. Is it really essential for each candidate for a vice-presidency to have had a stint in managing the factory at Podunk?

2. Use work-sharing, split-shift techniques for management positions so that opportunities to sharpen problem-attacking tools and develop responsible, decision-making skills are more widely extended to competent, motivated, younger married women.

• Develop modified, full-time positions, with lighter initial loads, to recruit, develop, and screen the younger women before their family and domestic demands have released them for full-time work.

• Redesign appropriate positions into a series of one-shot, single-problem assignments that are full time but temporary, and can be handled by a woman on a reduced-load basis similar to the method of farming out assignments to consulting or legal firms.

- Develop promising women candidates, who are not yet available for full-time management, through assignment of overflow management problems that presently overburden the full-time staff but are not sufficiently accumulated to necessitate a new, full-time position.[9]

Practical Considerations in Evaluating Her Opportunities

Women and companies should approach the creation of future opportunities for women in business as a cooperative venture. The woman has to be available; she has to be qualified; she has to meet the requirements of the job; and she must be a sound economic investment for the company. On the other hand, the company must be willing to accept, train, promote, and compensate her on a merit basis. It can recognize her slight limitations but at the same time capitalize on her tremendous potential.

It is worth noting that equality can, in some cases, be pushed too far. Women who demand equal opportunity for advancement may find themselves in a position of having to lift weights beyond their capabilities or of having to depend on muscle they just do not have. For example, six women employees of the Penn Central Railroad demanded their rights: They wanted the same opportunity for advancement as men had. They were promoted into the position of freight-car checkers, which involved climbing into and out of box cars all day. This back-breaking work was a means of advancement for men but was certainly not the kind of work suited to women.

Women must be prepared to accept and handle positions and responsibilities for which they insist on being trained and promoted. The company must live up to its responsibility by making available rights and benefits that it has led women to believe are attainable.

Current changes and trends indicate that both women and management are now being given the chance to exercise options that will provide equal opportunities for women and make their productive and management contribution available to help achieve the companies' goals. Women have to exercise the option of not selling themselves short, of being qualified for the job they seek, of adhering to the disciplines of the job, and of meeting job expectations. The company must exercise its options of selecting and promoting women on the basis of merit, of making all company resources accessible to her, and of taking advantage of the potential women represent.

[9] Estill Buchanan, "The Growing Opportunities for Women in Management," *Colorado Business Review* (University of Colorado, May 1968).

18

Conclusions

PERHAPS the single most significant error committed by men and management is that they tend to assume that all women are the same, that women are not individuals. They yield to the temptation of making decisions based on averages rather than on the merits of each individual woman. This has too often resulted in an inaccurate bench mark for women-oriented decision making. Their attitude is analogous to a doctor averaging the information on the charts at the foot of each bed in the hospital and prescribing cures based on the averages. This approach penalizes both the company and the women.

In attempting to evaluate working women, we must not use generalities as a basis for discriminating *against* women, but we must use sound judgment to be discriminating *about* them. Some conclusions can be drawn about working women:

They are capable of making an outstanding contribution to the profit goals of a company or the functional purposes of any group.

They are an important but underutilized human resource.

They are more family-oriented than men and are, therefore, subject to pressures and demands on their time, their energy, and their commitments.

Many women have different reasons for working than men which can influence quantitative performance and length of time they stay on the job.

The full potential of women will be realized only when uniquely appropriate leadership is supplied.

Harmony and improved results can be achieved with women if management deals objectively and realistically with potential problem areas such as length of employment, correction, attitudes, communication, and performance evaluation.

Women have demonstrated outstanding potential and competence for leadership at all levels; they deserve individual and objective consideration.

Trends indicate that, in the future, women will represent a larger percentage of the workforce in all areas and at all levels.

Women seek and deserve affirmation for themselves as individuals and for women as a sex. The record which each achieves either advances or impedes the progress of other women.

Women — properly employed, trained, supervised, compensated, promoted, and judged — represent the best bargain available to the company.

When all the numbers, percentages, and individuals have been fitted into place, management has but one inevitable course of action: to use to the maximum extent the current and future potential that women can offer the company.

Conclusions About Employing and Supervising Women

The company must first want to employ women and then back up this desire with changes and modifications in its recruitment and employment procedures. There is nothing so sacred about recruiting methods, testing procedures, interview techniques, criteria for employment, work schedules, position descriptions, compensation plans, and promotional policies that can't be changed to accommodate the hiring of women. For example, arrangements can be made so that two women, each available to work only four hours a day, can fill one full-time job. Or, minimum acceptable test scores can be adapted to recognize that a woman's lack of formal business or technical education may be compensated for by the amount of experience she's had in managing a home. When she seeks employment, let her know by what she sees and hears that she is welcome and that the company is an equal opportunity employer regarding sex.

All too often, discipline, rules, guides, and policies are in the "thou shalt" or "thou shalt not" category. Although women want a firm framework, they will often respond more positively to flexible leadership that bends to each new situation as it arises.

Women require the same kind of supervision as men, only more so. It is more important to comply with the rules of recognized good human relations. With women, it is more important to be fair, to communicate clearly, to correct objectively, to praise generously, to recognize achievement, and to maintain an attitude of understanding and patience.

If supervisors are sensitive and responsive to the subtle signposts women put up, they will be easier to supervise than men. Unfortunately, too many men fail to get the message, or they ignore it if they do.

Successful supervision is greatly influenced by first impressions, which are significant to a woman. Once she forms an attitude about something, it is difficult to change.

Supervision must provide a woman with the satisfaction she wants from her job. She needs a sense of belonging to the group, of having the approval of the supervisor, of having visible evidence of her progress, and of having a reasonable opportunity to feel that she is fulfilling her roles at home and on the job.

Common sense should be the guideline for encouraging, motivating, and implementing the contribution women can make. Their supervisor should not focus on the "female sex" but on each individual woman with her particular talents, abilities, and potential. Supervision should respond to people and to situations by providing the training, job environment, and leadership that can utilize the maximum potential of each woman.

Special Skills for Leadership of Women

Many men find it difficult to supervise women. They seem to handcuff themselves when it comes to taking action that involves their female subordinates. Yet it is the supervisor's responsibility to see that his department and his employees are functioning productively and efficiently. It would be well for supervisors to strengthen their abilities and skills in the following areas:

Communication. The supervisor must make all his communication with women clear and precise. Of equal importance are the attitudes of both sender and receiver. The communication must be meaningful to the receiver. It must identify precisely what action is expected of her and provide both the know-how and reasons for that expectation. Before responsive action can be taken, a relationship of mutual respect must exist. And both the woman and the supervisor must be willing to accept communication from each other.

Motivation. Women must understand how meeting job demands

made on them will fulfill their own needs. The link between performance and reward must be clear or women will not feel motivated.

Attitudes. The initial direction a woman's attitude takes and its permanent posture are influenced by her supervisor. Leadership must recognize its responsibility for the molding of attitudes and the significant effect that attitudes have on work achievement.

Correction. The job performance, not the performer, must be the focus of correction. Improved job performance and job-related activity offer the supervisor an opportunity to render a valuable service to his employees. If he performs his job skillfully, he improves the job security of the woman and increases her value to herself and to the company.

Job appraisal and improvement. It is imperative that management determine how well a woman is performing so that it can initiate all possible corrective action to maximize improvement.

Conclusions About Women's Leadership Potential

Effective leadership (whether by a man or a woman) demands a discipline, commitment, and quantitative orientation. Many women excel in these areas, but some are limited by home circumstances, lack of experience, or self-imposed restrictions on their career aspirations. A woman who enters the ranks of management is confronted with problems her male counterpart does not have: the fact that men are preferred to women as supervisors; traditional attitudes of male superiority and male dominance; and the reluctance of top management to provide training and positions for women. Women do, however, have certain advantages over men: a greater empathy and human insight; sincere feeling for the needs of people; and the mental ability required for leadership.

The Pendulum Swings in Her Favor

The current styles of management are particularly suited to the skills of women. The discovery of the outstanding achievement of team, persuasive, and humanistic leadership styles taps women's potential and gives them the opportunity to assume responsible roles.

Legal requirements should move women closer to equal opportunity, compensation, promotional consideration, and conditions of employment. Added to this are changes in job structure, physical requirements of work, social approval of working women, improved child-care facilities, decreased demands at home, and the shift toward more favorable attitudes of men and of management.

Women of today and tomorrow are preparing themselves for full-time careers by getting the education they need to obtain professional positions and by being willing to be judged on merit and to compete on equal terms with men.

A Final Judgment

If the problems of working women must be attributed to someone, much of the blame must rest on men, companies, and traditions that have unjustifiably restricted the opportunities of women. To a lesser degree, women themselves are to blame, especially those who have given less than their best effort, engaged in unprofessional job antics, and provided partial justification for the sometimes less than enthusiastic attitudes about women workers.

A final word: Women must seek employment and equal opportunity in the business environment as it exists today, not in the hoped-for or perfect state that hasn't arrived. If they wait for the red carpet to be rolled out, the open arms, and the welcome mat, they will have a long wait. They must assume sufficient initiative for being qualified, for seeking employment, for asking for equal opportunities regarding all conditions of employment.

Management must recruit, supervise, and utilize the womanpower that is available today. The longer management delays in getting its house in order and providing realistic equality for women, the more needless time and valuable potential will be wasted.

Appendixes

Appendix A

Results
of Author's Survey

BOTH men and women were questioned for this survey. Most of the women were managers, although secretaries, clerks, and housewives were included.

Almost one-third (32.5 percent) of the respondents were male. Seventy percent of the respondents were married, 16 percent were single, 12 percent divorced, and 2 percent widowed or separated. They had an average of 1.4 children. Eighty-seven percent of those responding supervised others; the average number of people supervised was 8.4.

Ninety-eight percent of the respondents thought that a special survey of the status, contributions, and unique circumstances of women in business was a valid work to undertake. One commented that there was "altogether too much misunderstanding" about the subject, and that "in far too many cases, facts have been tangled with emotions." Another thought the survey would "be helpful in formulating future plans and programs for the employment of women in positions that have heretofore been considered men's jobs." A third pointed out, "The male in business needs a lot of education on the subject," and still another respondent thought the survey might "make people more aware that a woman faces different problems from those of a man and that she perhaps works out these problems differently."

The survey revealed a wide range of feelings and opinions about women in business. They extended all the way from the obviously emotional belief that women are superior to men to the feeling that women are abjectly inferior. However, the majority of responses reflected the respondents' honest and conscientious effort to be informative and cooperative.

The amount and kind of personal experience respondents had in working

WHAT EFFECT SHOULD THE FOLLOWING ASSUMPTIONS HAVE ON
MANAGEMENT DECISIONS REGARDING EMPLOYMENT, PLACEMENT,
COMPENSATION, AND PROMOTION OF WOMEN? (*Results also shown in
Chapter 4.*)

	No Effect, percent	Significant Effect, percent	Disagree with Statement, percent
Women have a higher turnover rate in the 18–35 age bracket than men in the same age bracket	22	64	14
Women are absent more often than men	29	25	46
Women's medical, insurance, and other employee benefit costs are higher than men's	52	9	39
It's not wise to hire women because of the possible relocation or transfer of their husbands	41	57	2
The number and ages of children can keep women from their work	38	60	2
Both men and women are reluctant to accept supervision from women	52	31	17
The availability of women for travel and work off the premises is restricted	28	60	12
Women usually do not want transfers to other localities	31	61	8
A woman's age can affect her job performance	73	19	8
A husband working in the same company can be a problem	42	53	5
A married woman's job performance is different from a single woman's	75	20	5
Being a widow or divorcée can affect a woman's job performance	88	10	2
The position of a woman's husband affects her job	70	25	5

with women as employees or supervisors exerted a significant effect on their reactions. Those who had had little or no experience with women seemed to parrot prejudices about the deficiencies of female workers and leaders. Respondents more experienced with women workers invariably were more positive in their responses to the suitability and capability of women in the business world. Both men and women expressed some of the traditional uncertainties regarding women in business. They seemed to be concerned about women's dual roles of worker and housewife, the possible loss of femininity, the effect of work on women's home life, and tensions created when women compete with men.

The results of the survey will be shown by: (1) identifying the subject area or question, (2) using percentages and averages where numbers are involved, and (3) citing a cross section of direct quotes.

WHAT ADVANTAGES DO WOMEN HAVE OVER MEN?

As employees:

Better equipped temperamentally to handle certain types of detail-oriented jobs.
More perceptive to sensitive situations within office routine.
Capable women have the same advantages as capable men.
They have ways of getting what they want.
More adaptable to supervision.
None.
Flexibility, ability to identify with organization, a deep drive to be needed, capable of intense loyalty.

As supervisors:

In most cases, none.
Generally, they seem to be more sensitive to personal needs of employees.
Women's inborn ability to guide and direct efforts of others.
More imaginative, creative.
Greater sensitivity; better equipped to deal with problems of female employees.
Generally, more effective as trainers of employees.
More tolerant of employee frailties.
Better organizers; more ability to handle people: tact, softness, sensibility to situations and feelings of others.
More subtly persuasive, wider range of acting roles to use in accomplishing goals.

WHAT ADVANTAGES DO MEN HAVE OVER WOMEN?

As employees:

None, other than brawn.

No time out for child rearing.

More flexible in movement, travel, assignments; greater acceptance by the business community.

Less illness; work longer.

They get listened to more easily. They are given a chance more than a woman.

Accept change better.

Not as many outside influences.

They know when to keep their mouths shut and are better able to get the point—less emotional.

Less affected by personality clashes, generally capable of grasping the broader picture, less influenced by personal likes and dislikes.

Role as breadwinner insures their availability for continuous employment and development.

Less rivalry, more comradeship. Given most of the opportunities for advancement and leadership.

As supervisors:

Generally, they can cope with personnel problems better on an unemotional basis; better able to accept the long view.

No prejudice to overcome.

Are more relaxed and less demanding, given more respect and apt to stay on an even keel, less worry about home responsibilities.

Less resentment from people they are supervising. More objective and make decisions more quickly.

None, if women are as well trained as men.

Women will often confide in a man but not in a woman.

More often willing to work harder and longer; more anxious to improve themselves by outside work, reading, and the like.

More willpower, natural ability, and determination.

Doors are automatically open.

Less skeptical.

Essentially a better long-range investment—able to assume command at a younger age.

When a man is decisive, he evokes a father image; a woman is simply considered aggressive.

WHAT DISADVANTAGES DO WOMEN HAVE IN COMPARISON WITH MEN?

As employees:

None.
Receive lower pay for same work.
Not enough initiative. Historical social prejudices.
Require more or better supervision.
Women do not know when to mind their own business.
Not to act like a woman, but yet never let anyone forget that she is a woman.
Inability to win confidence of other women.
Some girls have the attitude that the job is only a "stopgap" prior to marriage or that the company is a "hunting ground."
It is assumed that they will be more emotional, unstable, less ambitious; that outside responsibilities will interfere and that strength will be limited.
Expect more comforts in working conditions.
Cliques — strong emotional involvement.
Not given authority to act to the same degree as men, lack of faith by men.

As supervisors:

Harder to supervise other women.
Lack of experience and training.
In nine out of ten cases, must do superior job — not average — to be accepted.
None of their mistakes are overlooked.
Have too much tendency to handle everything on a personal basis.
Harder to sell ideas to supervisors.
Ability to manage, be firm, and make immediate decisions.
Women don't like women by nature — personal jealousy.
Men — equals and subordinates — seem not to take a woman superior seriously. I sometimes feel they think I am playing a game and that my decisions are not necessarily binding.

IN WHAT AREAS ARE WOMEN SUPERIOR TO MEN?

As employees:

They seem better at dealing with people.
Faithful to job — delight in excellence.
Graciousness, warmth, compassion, tactfulness, and other human areas which might appear insignificant to men.

In jobs requiring patience and discrimination of fine details.
More thrifty and resourceful.
We're happy to finally be called equal; why push our luck and insist that
we are superior?
Women in confidential positions are less likely to leak information.

As supervisors:

None.
Use of tact and charm rather than force.
Sensitivity to interpersonal relationships; not hampered by fear of ap-
pearing soft.
Willingness for others to have the credit.
Hold their tempers better.
Willingness to see all sides of situations and to reconsider decisions.
Faster at spotting problems and pinpointing the exact nature of the
problem.
On jobs where great patience is needed and where intuition is important.
Department supervision as opposed to overall supervision.

WOULD YOU RATHER HAVE A STAFF COMPOSED
PRIMARILY OF MALES OR FEMALES?

Males: 36%   Females: 8%   No preference: 56%

Why male preference:

Just more used to how men think—can communicate more effectively
with men.
Fewer problems.
More stable and less emotional.
More candor, less pampering needed.
The complexity of women can and often does create problems that are
submerged or nonexistent in a male.
Difficulties in reprimanding women.

Why female or no preference:

I've supervised both—sex was no problem.
Balance created improved environment and productivity.
Depends on the job to be done and the skills and personal abilities re-
quired. I don't think you can generalize by sex.
I prefer females because they work better, work harder, have excellent
follow-through, have a genuine concern and enthusiasm.

DOES A WOMAN'S BUSINESS CAREER HAVE A MORE ADVERSE EFFECT
ON HER PERSONAL AND FAMILY LIFE THAN A MAN'S?

Yes: 58%   No: 42%
(Of the 42% who said "no," 24% were men and 76% women.)

Yes:

Usually a woman's major interest and responsibility is home and family.
   A man's career comes first.
She will neglect one or the other.
Business interferes only to the extent that she will allow it to.
Women's role of homemaker can't be filled with daytime absence.
She is still expected to do the housework, entertain, and participate in
   her husband's social commitments.

No:

A successful woman is able to manage her business career and her home
   career.
If it gives her satisfaction and monetary rewards, it should make her a
   more satisfied wife and mother.
Many marriages are strengthened because this makes the wife a better
   partner and guiding parent.
Women tend to separate careers from personal life more effectively than
   men, particularly if both are equally challenging.
If there is a proper understanding between husband and wife.

ARE THERE BUSINESS AREAS STILL BARRED TO WOMEN
BECAUSE OF THEIR SEX?

Yes: 64%   No: 36%
(Of those answering "yes," 83% were women, and only
17% were men. Of those answering "no," 46%
were women and 54% men.)

If yes, list barred areas:

In mechanical trades, mining, construction, and heavy production.
High executive levels in large corporations.
Industrial relations directors, purchasing managers, research managers,
   controllers, and many top management positions.
Perhaps not barred, but conspicuous by their absence.
Use of word "barred" too strong.
Hard physical labor for which she is not physically equipped.
Jobs involving extensive travel or climbing.

What are the areas in which women need to concentrate more effort in order to increase their overall effectiveness and contribution?

Dedication, initiative, tact, and patience—hard to come by when they are being ignored and passed over.

Emotional stability, objectivity in making decisions.

Increased training in motivation skills and objective analysis.

To change their own attitudes of inferiority and paranoia, to take a firmer and more positive stand on issues, and to get more education above the high school and business school level.

Ability to accept challenge of new ideas and bring mature viewpoint as against purely feminine viewpoint to the job.

Must learn to accept criticism as a means of future development.

Let the other person think it's his idea if that's the only way to get a good program started.

What unique assets or contributions do you think women are able to make to business?

Because of their homemaking instinct, women have contributed to a more comfortable and acceptable work environment.

Intuitiveness, practicality, ability to envision results for long-range objectives.

A fine sensitivity which gives them a perspective that many men lack.

Constructive criticism, a woman's point of view on supervision, administration, personnel relations, and management.

Nothing unique—let's just say they complement or round out the situation. Men are best at some things and women at others.

It is possible that women may improve the ethical and moral implications of getting a job done.

What factors in business make it difficult for women to advance to higher levels?

She can't go and play golf or have a drink with the men; much of executive life revolves around "men only" activities.

Men, in general, are afraid of competent and intelligent women if they are in same promotion lineup.

Age-old prejudices that women are not intellectually or emotionally suited for executive capacities.

Seniority requirement.

Less time to accumulate knowledge on which to advance than comparable men.

Women cannot be expected to pick up at a moment's notice and be away from home for several days.

WHAT CHANGES WOULD IMPROVE WOMEN'S OPPORTUNITIES FOR ADVANCEMENT TO HIGHER BUSINESS LEVELS?

Women must learn to keep bitterness out of their attitude; men must evaluate women by ability, not sex.

I know of nothing that will change the fact that executive-level jobs demand a great deal of time devoted to the job, and most women hope to marry and rear a family.

Adding women to management training programs so other employees are put on notice that they are being considered.

Grown-up behavior by women in business.

Let's not change it.

WHAT TYPES OF TRAINING WOULD PROVE MOST BENEFICIAL TO WOMEN?

As employees:

Careful preparation for the job—incentives and rewards for excellence.

More technical training—sober objective courses, not arts, crafts, and marriage.

Learning to understand and accept constructive criticism, and to act as a professional woman.

Training to build her confidence in her own ability.

As supervisors:

Basic management training.

Knowledge and skill in interpersonal relationships—leadership courses.

Opportunity to get same training as men.

A course directed at teaching her to gain the respect of co-workers, subordinates, and superiors.

WHAT IS THE MOST EFFECTIVE KIND OF SUPERVISION TO USE IN MANAGING WOMEN?

From men supervisors:

Gentle, but firm. Men must supervise women impersonally.

Believe in them; let them know that you respect their brains and ability; trust them; treat them as mature people; don't tolerate immaturity in them.

Fairness. Show no favoritism.

Depends on the individual, not the sex.

If women demonstrate their ability, just point them in the right direction. Results will astound the boss.

Treating them as equals with respect to knowledge and business.

Sympathetic but consistent.

Tactful request for assistance rather than pressure for urgency.

From women supervisors:

Distant, firm, cool.

Don't try to be one of the girls.

Respect their ability, assist, but do not "overly boss"; keep relationship as impersonal as possible; do not tolerate irresponsibility.

Firm—almost dictatorial.

As unemotional as possible.

Must learn to compliment and commend female employees.

Equality, not condescension.

Retain femininity while assuming masculine attitudes.

Must be firm with younger women and lead older women.

HAS THE EQUAL-PAY LAW AND PROHIBITION AGAINST SEX
DISCRIMINATION IN THE CIVIL RIGHTS LAW AFFECTED
THE STATUS AND OPPORTUNITIES FOR WOMEN?

Yes: 70.5%   No: 20.9%   Other: 8.9%

Some, but not as much as it can. Women's own fault.

It opens the thinking about possible infringement. Direct financial adjustments—my own salary was adjusted. (From a female respondent.)

More jobs and higher earning are now possible, although the changes are coming slowly.

A woman simply cannot afford to challenge the issue; it will immediately prove what men have said all along—"emotional, nit-picker, etc."

Forced employers to think in terms of larger responsiblities for women.

As a practical matter, I doubt it.

Business does not accept mandate.

But only at nonexempt levels.

The respondents were asked to state their reactions to the following statements:

"WOMEN TALK TOO MUCH."

Only some scattered few who spoil it for all women.

It is true that women show emotional traits not apparent in men.

Nonsense, I know as many talkative men as women.

This emotion is the "steam" that makes them valuable employees.

Any successful woman knows that the way to a man's ego is to let him talk about himself.

Give them more opportunities to perform and they will talk less.

"WOMEN ARE TOO EMOTIONAL."

True, but women are learning to control this—if they want to get ahead.
No more than men, they just show it in a different way.
No, emotions are important to a well-balanced person. True, there are a
few who go overboard.
Watch it!
Women may be more emotional than men but probably have fewer ulcers.
I've seen male managers blow their tops, allow themselves to be manipu-
lated, get away with incompetence that wouldn't be tolerated in a woman.
True. A woman is made of emotion.

"WOMEN CAN'T KEEP THINGS CONFIDENTIAL."

Not true. But very often, while they are trying desperately to keep things
confidential, it comes back to them from male sources.
Nonsense. The biggest rumor mongers I know are male executives.
When I need to tap the grapevine, I go to a man.
Unfortunately, true in many instances.

"WOMEN ARE TOO SUBJECTIVE AND INTUITIVE IN THEIR THINKING, REACTING, AND DECISION MAKING."

True. They must be trained in objective management.
Sometimes this is a big advantage and brings about different solutions.
Perhaps so, but women are good barometers for office morale.
No more so than men. A woman's intuition is often quite correct.
Most good women bend over backward to be objective. Intuition is a fine
quality when used correctly by men or women.
Aren't these the traits we expect from top managers?
Female intuition stems from sensitivity to feelings and reactions of others.

"WOMEN ARE TOO CONCERNED WITH SMALL DETAILS TO MANAGE MAJOR RESPONSIBILITIES."

Untrue. They are often given small details as work instead of major re-
sponsibilities to manage, thus breeding attention to detail.
Nonsense! They are filling the vacuum left by the men.
Training and orientation can change this.
They are overly detail-minded; this is an area in which they need help.

"WOMEN ARE TOO CONCERNED WITH THEIR APPEARANCE."

Hooray!
Would men have it any other way?
Have yet to see where this is a disadvantage in relation to either sex.

As a general rule, this is untrue and seldom undesirable unless it detracts their attention from the job.

A woman must of necessity do more than comb her hair to keep from being considered sloppy.

I can hear the complaints if we weren't.

"WOMEN WORRY TOO MUCH ABOUT WHAT OTHER PEOPLE MIGHT THINK."

Any insecure person—man or woman—worries about what others think. Women do not have a monopoly on worry.

This is true with the majority.

A good female executive doesn't.

Not me!

Women are concerned about what others might think, but once secure in a position, this diminishes.

"WOMEN ARE TOO JEALOUS OF EACH OTHER."

More overtly so than men, but men can be just as nasty about it.

After watching and listening to the battles of my male peers, I've learned women have no monopoly on jealousy.

I have always felt loyalties given to women, by women, would benefit both.

Women just find it harder to conceal.

True. Their worst trait insofar as making real progress in the business world.

This kind of woman should not be an executive.

"WOMEN ARE TOO LIKELY TO 'GET IT IN' FOR SOMEONE ELSE."

No more than men.

Ridiculous. For the most part, I think women are more tolerant.

Yes, it is a natural trait with so many.

Never!

Yes, but men do this also in more devious ways.

"WOMEN TAKE EVERYTHING PERSONALLY."

Life is personal. In order to do a good job, it must be taken personally.

Some do. They are not thick-skinned enough.

Has been true, but as women get more experience in business, they are not doing this as much.

Not unless reflection on herself; admitted weakness.

Women are more sensitive than men probably are, but this very quality makes them valuable members of an organization if this quality is recognized and built on.

Everyone has days when they take things wrong.

If you deal fairly with women, there is little personal feeling involved.

"WOMEN ARE TOO INCONSISTENT."

Unfair statement.

Consistency or lack of consistency varies with individuals, not sex.

Not as much as men. Often women have been said to be inconsistent when they are actually trying to please a changeable male boss.

Definitely not a female prerogative. If anything, tend to lean on consistency too hard when some bending or inconsistency might be just what's needed.

Yes, but dependable when the chips are down.

"WOMEN ARE MORE DIFFICULT TO SUPERVISE."

No. I supervise 48 people, 9 women and 39 men. I don't have anywhere near the problems with the women that I have with about 8 of the men.

Not as long as they are treated fairly and equally.

Women require better supervision. They tend not to overlook careless supervision as men will.

False. I don't know any boss who has said this after working with women employees.

True, maybe because financial security is less important to men. Women can exercise more independent judgment, which creates supervisory problems.

Mainly a problem of personalities and home environment.

Women are not more difficult to supervise but must be supervised differently.

Not if they are praised occasionally and are aware of goals to be met.

"WOMEN ARE TOO DEFENSIVE."

I suppose the answers on this survey are proof positive that this is true.

Have they not been given cause to be defensive?

Agreed. She doesn't know how else to preserve her job status.

So are many men.

They have been put on the defensive by the attitude: "You can't be in charge, you're a woman!" Accept a woman for her worth, and usually the overdefensiveness will disappear.

Most are very conscious of this.

Phooey!

"WOMEN HAVE TO CHOOSE BETWEEN HOME AND CAREER; THEY CAN'T BE GOOD AT BOTH."

Women have proved that they can be effective both at home and in a career.

Can manage a job and have a happy home with well-adjusted children. It is largely an understanding between husband and wife.

Can't be good at one unless they are good at the other.

Can a man? It depends on the person, entirely.

Can't buy this. Takes a little more finesse is all! I have been much more effective at home since I started a career—now make better use of time, really enjoy family more, more confidence and compatibility.

They can be good at both, but excel in only one.

Why shouldn't they be good at both? All it takes is organization and the ability to devote wholehearted attention to each at the appropriate times. Variety can keep a woman alert and more interesting.

This is very true.

"A WOMAN MUST BE TWICE AS COMPETENT AS A MAN IF SHE IS TO COMPETE."

Women must be more capable than men in order to secure and hold the same level position.

Indeed not! Competence is competence.

On the same level, yes.

There are some built-in prejudices against them, so there's certainly some truth to this.

A mediocre male will be given the benefit of a doubt, but a woman will be discounted.

Absolutely true!

Unfortunately, to batter down the doors of the executive tower, this is true; but I hope she does not become masculine in manner.

Right, but surely this is going to change.

IN WHAT WAYS WILL THE ROLE OF WOMEN CHANGE IN THE FUTURE?

As employees:

Women will be brought up from childhood to seek careers as men do, rather than temporary jobs between school and family.

Somewhere along the line, men are going to learn that *all* women shouldn't be described as they were by some of the statements in this survey.

More wives will return to the work world after their children are of school age.

The need to help out at home in financial matters is causing more women to seek employment.

There will be fewer jobs held by only men or only women.

Managers of the future will evaluate employees without regard to sex or color.

I think they are going to demand more representation.

As they get more experience, women are becoming better employees; and they are being trained for all types of work.

They will go as far as they are willing to.

As supervisors:

The shortage of male supervisors, as well as bright, young management men, will make it imperative to change attitudes.

Must be developed by training geared to women.

Will be considered first for supervisory departments where the workforce is primarily women.

Hopefully will become more accepted and can spend more time getting the job done rather than proving herself.

The barriers will crumble, but oh, so slowly, I fear.

More women employees with good education will force management to use its capabilities.

As to types of jobs:

In many cases, women will have to aggressively seek the types of jobs they desire from their employers.

Those requiring great physical effort and great scientific knowledge will never be filled by women.

Hopefully more in management, but have a long way to go as to salary.

Women will be equal to men in jobs requiring brains but not brawn.

Training more women for EDP and systems work. Do an excellent job and will not move as readily as men.

A greater spectrum of jobs should be open to women because predictions indicate there will not be a sufficient number of men to fill them.

If a woman has an interest in a field, it will be open to her.

As to levels of responsibility:

Great potential in areas of working with people.

Analyzing and understanding society and its values; resolving conflicts by personal adjustments.

Depends on whether a woman comes to realize that she, like a man, lives in a world characterized by opportunity and choice. Her own preferences and the demands made on her, if she aspires to professional status, will require long years of training.

I emphasize that there should be training for women supervisors, and I do not think this training should be in a separate group from men. They should be trained together.

As prejudice and false tales vanish more, women will surge to the top.

They can achieve any level of responsibility if they educate and train themselves — and if it is the policy of an organization to recognize the abilities of a woman and promote her accordingly.

Pay scales, better education, and legal pressures will force consideration of women in higher levels of responsibilities.

Here are some additional comments volunteered by the respondents:

Contrary to what some men think, we don't want to be "one of the boys." We just feel we should have equal opportunity (and equal pay) based on ability and merit. . . . But we are wasting a lot of talent in the meantime.

The survey appears to come from a woman's civil liberties group rather than from a male executive. It is slanted too heavily toward the demands of those advocating equal rights for women. The woman trying to go into areas above her capacity tries one's patience.

I sincerely feel that the attitude to take should be "Can this individual person do the job I need done regardless of whether male or female?"

Women are still their own worst enemies, but aren't all people? They want equality but, as a group, haven't been willing to earn it.

I firmly believe many executives (men) are successful because of the help they've received from their women assistants and secretaries. The ladies do the work and often furnish the "brainpower" for the man who ultimately receives the reward. I believe the credit should be given where it is due and should be rewarded accordingly.

The big difference in ability shows when women get hung up on a disaster or crisis. The capable man or woman immediately goes to work on a solution while others are still sputtering or defending themselves. Women must learn to think like men on the job and bring the special female qualities along as a charming dividend.

Sex attitudes will continue to make the male feel dominant (even when he isn't) and the female seductive (even when she isn't) for many generations at least. Sex discrimination is more subtle, more widespread, and less recognized by men than race discrimination.

If there is mass unemployment, we will likely hear of the woman's place as being in the home.

Men and women must work in partnership, each contributing his or her unique abilities to realize mutually agreed-upon goals.

Women must not be shunted aside as inferiors in big business. If recognition is merited, it must be given.

Tradition is hard to overcome, but business can no longer achieve its goals and this country can no longer maintain its economic growth without women taking a substantial role in business. "It's a man's world" is done for.

The major problem for women is the prejudice and lack of acceptance by those who are not objective. Ability is not a sex characteristic.

CONCLUSIONS

The survey demands a repetition of the statement that "neither men nor women are neutral where women are concerned." Survey questions were designed to give the respondents an opportunity to express their feelings, opinions, attitudes, and prejudices. The following conclusions can be drawn:

The answers of males and females were usually different and easy to identify.

Men's reactions were the opposite of women's reactions to the same statements.

Men still exhibit a considerable amount of subjective thinking where women are concerned.

Women still feel that the attitudes of men constitute their biggest stumbling block on the road to equal job opportunity, equal pay, and successful executive leadership.

There was a consensus of both sexes that more education, better training, self-development, increased ambition, and better self-image are necessary to accelerate the progress of women.

The very denials, defenses, emotional reactions, and hostile answers were confirmation of attitudes the answers sought to refute.

There was general agreement by both sexes that vast amounts of potential womanpower at all skill levels are being wasted because of social traditions, prejudices, archaic company policies, inadequate or inappropriate job preparation, and male-oriented company structures.

Both sexes acknowledged the presence of stereotyped ideas and job-related differences in men and women. But both also agreed that these differences are not too significant and that the merit of the individual, not the sex, should be the overriding influence.

Both men and women seemed genuinely sincere in wanting to advance the job opportunity and progress of women.

Women, for the most part, were hopeful that the survey and its results would identify some of the problems they confront, thereby contributing to their solutions.

The survey revealed considerable information regarding the ways in which women see themselves. Many are ambitious and feel confident that they can skillfully manage their roles as wives, mothers, homemakers, and careerists all at the same time. Perhaps most importantly, executives of both sexes revealed their present thinking regarding women employees and leaders as well as what they think should be done to enlarge the future opportunities for women at all levels of society and in all kinds of companies.

Appendix B

Point of View:
An Interview
with Female Executives

THIS is a verbatim transcript of excerpts from a two-hour discussion between the author and a group of women executives. The group was assembled for the sole purpose of discussing women in business. They were told at the beginning that the session would be tape-recorded. The group was composed of:

> The director of industrial relations for a manufacturing plant.
> The director of vocational education for a large city-county school system.
> The vice-president of a statewide bank.
> The supervisor of a civil service office with the United States government.
> The vice-chancellor of a major state university.
> The personnel executive of a financial institution.
> The manager of a newspaper advertising department.
> The director of a university school of nursing.

Do you think that a discussion regarding women in business can be of benefit?

PANELIST: Yes, very definitely. There is a big gap between the understanding men and women have of each other in business. It is the fault of the culture. I've always felt that men and women live in two different worlds because they're reared that way. Women very often are accused of being emotional. It's more the fact that the male and female are taught to respond differently. So maybe this discussion will help each to understand the other a little better.

PANELIST: I think this discussion and book about the results are extremely important. It's not difficult to contemplate the importance of it when you consider the high percentage of women in the working world.

PANELIST: Women have yet to reach their proper level of opportunity in business. It's only through surveys or meetings or various other media that we are finally going to receive the recognition we should have. If we don't do something about it ourselves, I don't think anyone else is going to do it for us.

Michelet stated, "Nearly every folly committed by women is born of the stupidity of man."

PANELIST: Agreed.

PANELIST: I'm not sure that men as a whole are aware of this. They don't recognize that they are prejudiced against women — at least, they don't like to admit it. I'm not sure they recognize the problems we have in trying to overcome these barriers.

PANELIST: Don't you think it depends entirely upon the age of the male? The younger men seem to be more prejudiced against women than men who have been in the business world for some time.

PANELIST: I'd say that age is a factor, and that would go back again to our culture and the total picture of our society, which has been one of men leading for so many years in the executive jobs and higher positions.

PANELIST: I believe that the man who has more experience in working with women is much more willing to take a viewpoint that enables women to reach higher management levels.

What about the question of a higher turnover rate for women in the eighteen to thirty-five age bracket?

PANELIST: It has not been so with my company. There is a higher turnover with men, expecially in the eighteen to thirty-five bracket.

PANELIST: I'd like to take the other side of that. People in research and personnel people say that this *is* a significant factor.

PANELIST: I'm sure it is. We may have a unique situation, but I can only speak of what's true in our own organization. I know "why" we have less turnover in our women. It's because there are very few places that women can earn as much money as they do with us.

What about higher absenteeism? Is this true of women employees?

PANELIST: Yes.

PANELIST: Can you make generalities so wide and sweeping on this kind of thing? What may be very true in some part of our profession may not be at all true in others.

PANELIST: If you have a husband and wife who are employed and making approximately the same salary the mother is going to stay home when her child is sick.

PANELIST: I think that women make the mistake of thinking that they can do a full day's work and still do everything at home that they would do if they were not working. They do two jobs while men do one.

PANELIST: I would have to argue with that in some instances. I have friends whose husbands do just as much of the housework as the wives do.

PANELIST: A high percentage of traveling salesmen leave on Monday morning and don't come back until Friday. So there are women who are working who have families, all of the housework to do, and every other responsibility for five days a week.

Do you think the point might arrive, ten or fifteen years from now, when the same number of men and women will be leaving for five days of travel each week?

PANELIST: It could be, but I don't know how a mother could leave her children.

PANELIST: I don't think you could ever divorce women completely from their family responsibilities.

Is it true that women have higher medical and insurance costs?

PANELIST: It's true, but it shouldn't be.

PANELIST: We've had an odd situation. I made a breakdown some twelve to fifteen years ago, and our medical costs were higher for men. But today they're more than twice as high for women. Again, I don't know whether this is because of the low turnover rates of our women. They've been with us longer, so it might be natural to have more health problems.

PANELIST: I supervise just women, and I don't find this to be particularly true. I have the age group where you would expect more hospitalization. Yet, when I look around the building, the men are the ones having the heart attacks and staying out for three or four months at a time. If a woman is out, it's only for three or four days, and then she's back at work.

PANELIST: I think you're expressing a basic truth—that women go into the hospital more often but stay a shorter period of time, while men have illnesses less often but require longer periods of hospitalization.

What about the possibility of relocation and transfer of the husband as it might affect the employment and placement of women?

PANELIST: If it does not require too much training for her to perform effectively on the job, I don't think you should hesitate to employ her.

PANELIST: Where the company might invest a lot of money in her, it would have some effect on whether or not you might employ that person.

PANELIST: I don't think you would have as many women applying for the kinds of jobs where you would be investing a lot of money in training. They tend to apply for jobs where the cost of training is considerably less.

PANELIST: I do think that on a long-term investment basis a woman just out of college is not as good an investment as a young man. I say it, in all fairness, for this reason: At that age, she's very likely to marry and leave. Of course, the man might leave too. But I do think that the economic factor has to be taken into consideration when you are training for a high-level job.

PANELIST: Don't you think that most women, when they finish college and go to work, say they will work for just a certain number of years whereas the man knows he will be working for the rest of his life? So, certainly, he's a better investment.

At what age is a woman the best investment?

PANELIST: Thirty-five and up.

PANELIST: Companies are beginning to realize that this is a good age.

Is this the age level training should be aimed at? And should companies be willing to place a woman of this age in junior executive and technical training programs?

PANELIST: Right. This is your best bet, in my opinion. People are marrying younger. By the time a woman is thirty-five, she is either going to face a very empty life and feel unneeded, or she's going back into the labor market. A good many of them are college graduates and well trained. To me, this is the best bet to hire for executive and junior executive positions.

PANELIST: Sometimes whether or not the youngster goes to college depends on the mother's income. So she has a great deal at stake. She's anxious to earn as much money as she can just as quickly as she can, and she will apply herself more.

PANELIST: Maturity is so valuable. You don't need the firmness in supervising and directing the more mature woman that you need with a young person. Unless you hold a very firm hand on a young woman, she has too many outlets in which she can go and not produce. Whereas with a mature person, they want leadership and accept it more easily. It isn't necessary to push and drive and stay with them so much of the time.

PANELIST: Most people at that age have a better understanding of themselves, which is absolutely essential before you can really accomplish goals that you set.

PANELIST: If a woman at that age returns to the labor market, she and her husband will have already built their marriage. They have settled into their marriage, and the husband doesn't mind too much.

PANELIST: Also, today, women at thirty-five are much younger than women at thirty-five were twenty years ago. I think the health factor enters in here. And I think that people are living longer and having better health so that you can expect a longer term of employment.

Do you think that women lack the confidence to do a job comparable to a man's?

PANELIST: You hit the nail on the head when you say it's a lack of confidence. Man has always been, and probably always will be, the aggressor. His natural inclination would be that a man can do the job better than a woman. This could be frustrating to a woman who thinks or knows she can do a better job than a man can.

PANELIST: I think women often conform to the expectations men have of them in business.

PANELIST: Do you think the woman's philosophy might be, "Blessed is she who expects nothing and then she won't be disappointed"? I think the attitude of "women versus men" has gone out of fashion. It's more a matter of a team rather than the women over here on this side and the men over there on that side.

PANELIST: I think women have a lot of changing to do in their thinking, too. Women have been brought up to think that there are certain jobs that are women's and certain jobs that are men's. Some women break that pattern and realize that they are individuals and people before they are women. But there are many of them who don't. This is where you need a lot of reeducation as far as the women are concerned.

What are the problems that women have with women?

PANELIST: They know them too well.

PANELIST: In many cases a woman employee can get by with things that a man can't.

PANELIST: I think one of the most difficult things in supervising women is that you can't help liking certain people more than others. It is difficult to be absolutely impartial to each person, even though you know that this person is doing an excellent job and making money for your company—while another person is just as important, but is just a slow starter. Eventually, she may be just as valuable as the first, but you still have a tendency to like the first one better because she produces more.

PANELIST: I find that it is a little difficult not to push things the way of the person who is actually producing more.

Wouldn't a man be just as likely to do that?

PANELIST: I think he very definitely would, but probably not to the extent a woman would, because I think that I'm a little bit more sensitive than a man would be in the same job. I can gauge the moods a little better than he can, and women wear their feelings a little closer to the surface than men do.

PANELIST: I think this has improved greatly.

PANELIST: We have a more stable female.

PANELIST: Well, we've had a "shorter term of office," so to speak, in the business world. I think women entered it unsure of themselves, and I think World War II did much to eliminate this. A lot of women went to work during the war for patriotic reasons, and then they suddenly realized that they could do a job. I think they were just as surprised as anyone else. And then they found that in addition to a pay check, they got a good deal of self-satisfaction out of it. They're just beginning to find themselves.

PANELIST: Well, women are better educated and better trained than they were twenty or twenty-five years ago. A supervisor, to do an efficient job, must be a leader of people. This, in itself, can create some problems with both men and women. But you can cope with this by being objective. I think the supervisor of either women or men must be superior, perhaps to some degree in intelligence, to do this well.

Do you think a woman must be better and more intelligent and do a better supervisory job under the same circumstances than a man?

PANELIST: I think this is true. But I think they can do it.

PANELIST: I think age makes a lot of difference. If an older person is supervising younger people, then the younger people have respect for the person and feel she is going to be a better supervisor than a supervisor closer to their own age.

PANELIST: Getting back to expectations, I'd like to know how many women in this room expected to reach an executive status when they went to work? I didn't.

PANELIST: Neither did I.

PANELIST: This is what I'm talking about—that women need a lot of training so that they can learn what they are capable of and what they can do. I thought if I got a job as a secretary, I had it made!

PANELIST: When a woman goes to work, she goes to work to teach or to be a secretary. But women don't think in terms, as men do, of having a goal of an executive-level job.

PANELIST: I think the trend in continuing education is going to influence this.

PANELIST: Women must accept the idea that they've got to keep going to school in order to get higher positions.

PANELIST: I do think that a woman has to be smarter; she has to *be* there; she has to be better educated in order to hold the same position that "he" does.

Would you say that a man can get along more easily by doing a less effective job of supervision?

PANELIST: Very definitely.

PANELIST: I don't think so, not anymore. Men may get by for a while, but I don't think they're going to get by over a long period of time.

PANELIST: Well, I'd say they have to meet a certain standard of efficiency. But I think it is true that a woman has to go beyond the accepted standard to get ahead.

PANELIST: Management looks toward the man and, as long as results are achieved, it doesn't pick at small things.

In the so-called professional management concept that's in vogue today—where you have goals and objectives and standards—do you think that the focus will be more and more on results produced rather than the individual in that job, whether it be male or female?

PANELIST: Yes, very definitely.

What influence do you think management by results will have on the opportunity of women?

PANELIST: It will increase women's expectations when they go on a job, which is very important.

PANELIST: And when the name comes out on the computer card, it will have initials, and it may not be known whether it's a male or female.

PANELIST: I'd like to say that there's one other attitude men have that comes from good intentions but has bad results. I think it's an overly protective attitude that men have toward women, that there are still some harsh realities that men just don't think women should have to deal with. I run into this every once in a while.

You mean that men are overprotective of women in the business world?

PANELIST: Well, may I give you just an example? We had two men get into a fight, and it would have been my job to settle it; but they didn't think I should come in contact with this unpleasantness. This is what I mean by good intentions. When Title VII came into effect with the women in the plant, we had to decide which jobs would be open to men and women and which ones had to remain strictly male jobs. We had a management meeting and one of the top executives said, "But women will get dirty doing that."

Do you feel that men should be less protective of women?

PANELIST: I certainly do. I think that women should meet all the standards of the job, or they shouldn't have it.

And if they can meet those standards — mentally, emotionally, physically — they should have equal opportunity for the job?

PANELIST: That's right. But no exceptions, no making the job easier. To do this is a little insulting in a way.

Do women have unique or special interests or needs that relate to the job?

PANELIST: I think that if things are more pleasing with the walls blue rather than pink, paint them blue. If the color has something to do with performance on the job, fine! Change it. If it has nothing to do with the results obtained, I wouldn't care at all.
PANELIST: I think it would make more difference to a woman than a man whether the wall is a particular color.
PANELIST: I tell you, I've seen a man so picky . . .

Is the social environment more important to a woman than to a man?

PANELIST: I think so.
PANELIST: I don't know.
PANELIST: We have a young man at our bank on the management training program who brought up something that I had never thought about. He said that an employer should offer his employees the opportunity to work with the people they would enjoy working with.
PANELIST: I think that's true of anybody, man or woman. But I think that women have more concern with being needed personally. I believe the "human" does come into a woman's work more.
PANELIST: I think that males and females have the same need there. Males may not express it as much as females.

PANELIST: I think women tend to be more inconsistent than men.

PANELIST: They're more emotional.

PANELIST: I don't know whether they are or not.

PANELIST: I disagree with both. They're emotional in different ways. Men blow their tops and women cry, but both are emotional outlets — just different means of expression.

PANELIST: I find that women have a tendency to hit the heights and the depths more than men do. In other words, there are smaller things that are more important to the woman than there are to the man, at least in the group I supervise.

PANELIST: For instance, if someone on the detail desk speaks rather sharply to one of the girls, her feelings are hurt, and she comes and tells me about it. I think that if we'd had a man on the desk, he wouldn't think anything of it.

PANELIST: I think he would feel like kicking back just like the woman would.

PANELIST: Well, he probably would, but he wouldn't go tell somebody else.

PANELIST: He would probably think that it was petty to come to a woman supervisor and say, "Look, this girl over here said something to me."

PANELIST: You'd think he was an old maid.

PANELIST: He'd probably think of himself as an old maid more than thinking it was all right that he come and complain.

What about the dual role of homemaker and working woman? It's been said that a woman cannot be good in both areas.

PANELIST: I think that she can today. It doesn't require half as much effort to be a good homemaker today as it did ten or twenty years ago. Women have so much time and so much valuable talent. They're in every level of work and they're doing top-flight jobs. And they're being good homemakers too. I believe we can make excuses that you can't do both, but we have too many examples of people who *are* doing both.

Would it be just as reasonable to make the statement that a man cannot be good in both areas — husband, father, and businessman?

PANELIST: No, I don't think they're strong enough. (Laughter.)

PANELIST: Many fathers bring their problems to work with them. They are concerned about the children who are home ill, but they seldom worry about their daughter's long gloves for debutante parties.

PANELIST: It isn't the quantity of time spent with the child, it's the quality. And I think a child is much better off with a working mother who is fulfilling her needs and is happy than with a mother who resents the fact that she is home and feels that she does not have any sense of personal achievement whatsoever.

PANELIST: I also think that very often she makes a better wife because she has a better understanding of her husband's problems when he comes home. And she doesn't meet him at the door with all the little petty things that have happened. She grows as he grows.

PANELIST: This is most important too.

PANELIST: Well, she has a complete separate life that should be very interesting to him, just as his separate life is interesting to her. They have a lot more communication, a lot more things to talk about than they would have if the woman stays at home.

In Betty Friedan's book, The Feminine Mystique, *there is a basic idea that women are searching for meaning and status.*

PANELIST: I think this is true. It's true mainly because making a home is no longer a full-time job. The woman used to be the hub of the universe as far as her home was concerned. But now children have different interests; they have more outside activities. The husband has different interests. She has nothing but that house, and she can spend the rest of her days playing bridge or some such thing; but it is not a satisfactory life. When our mothers came along, homemaking was a real challenge.

PANELIST: I think most of the young women who enter the labor market early in their marriage when there are very young children in the home do so for economic reasons rather than to fulfill their needs.

PANELIST: In this age group, yes, but not when women are thirty-five or over.

PANELIST: I think most young mothers need to be with their children for a few years. The children need them, and I think the mother misses a lot and the children miss a lot. But sometimes mothers *have* to go to work.

PANELIST: One thing that I think is good is that I see a lot of young mothers now who just finished high school. And, while their children are young, they go back to college at night. They are with the children in the daytime, but when those children are old enough for her to leave, she's trained and ready to step into a good job. She has a full life and has enough outside interests to keep her aware of things.

Is this search for meaning unique to the woman?

PANELIST: No, and I think men really have one handicap here — they are still the head of the house and the breadwinners. If they are unhappy in their job, they are "stuck" with it. They have to compromise.

PANELIST: They don't have the same freedom women have to move into something they'd rather do. They may even sometimes compromise to a large degree at a higher-level job because they are still the main support of the family.

PANELIST: This is one of the weaknesses in working women—the fact that many of them feel that theirs is a second income and they can quit whenever they like. Therefore, you have more turnover.

PANELIST: We had one woman leave, and she said, "Well my husband said I could get another job." So she did.

PANELIST: But whether they leave and go to another job or whether they are in the home, they are still searching for one thing, I think. And that's identity.

Well, what sort of identity are they searching for?

PANELIST: The feeling that they're needed to render a service and that they're important.

PANELIST: I suppose they want to do good. But take the nursing profession. You don't find too many Florence Nightingales who just want to serve mankind.

PANELIST: I do think that we are motivated by whatever we think will make us feel good or give us some satisfaction.

What advice would you give men who supervise women?

PANELIST: To accept her as an individual first and a woman second.

PANELIST: I think because of the insecurity built up when they first start to work—and our culture—that women need a lot of praise and a lot of acceptance.

PANELIST: I don't think she has as much self-confidence in the business world as a man. It's going to take several generations to correct that.

PANELIST: It's changing rapidly, but she still has a long way to go.

PANELIST: Insecurity. There's something about that word that I can't comprehend. I've never felt insecure. I can't feel that a secretary or anybody coming into a job with a good educational background—plus the fact that she's going to be trained for that job—should feel insecure.

PANELIST: I think a person who is insecure at eighteen is also insecure twenty years later. I think the aging process does not always overcome insecurities.

PANELIST: I think that male supervisors must be objective at all times in terms of their personal feelings about an individual. I think that men tend to favor the rapid producer, the quick learner, and the more sophisticated woman.

PANELIST: I think a lot has to do with expectation. I know there were many times when my supervisor would call me into his office and say, "We need to do this or that." I'd go back and mull it over and I'd think, "Great Scott, he must be out of his mind. I can't even begin

PANELIST: to do this." And then I'd think, "If he thinks that I can do it, some-how or other I will." I think this is where men fail a great deal. They don't throw the challenge out to women enough.

PANELIST: You've really got a good point there. I think that it's really not direct supervision; it's giving goals, setting objectives.

PANELIST: This is true of any supervisor, male or female. One of the basic keys to good supervision is to make people feel that you have confidence in them when they may not even have that confidence in themselves. People reach beyond their ability if you give them enough of your confidence. Give them a challenge.

PANELIST: Don't you think that supervisors should let their women know more about what's going on — in other words, fully inform them so that they can feel a real part of the institution rather than just going there and putting in eight hours a day and not really knowing what their efforts are achieving?

I heard a speaker say recently, "Motivation is primarily involvement."

PANELIST: Right, exactly right.

PANELIST: Many times you have to push a person toward this involvement.

PANELIST: We're always talking about training. How much training do we have for women supervisors? Isn't there a great need for this kind of training?

PANELIST: Well, we have just recently opened our executive training program to women as well as men. So I feel very encouraged that women are now being accepted.

If we were to draw significant conclusions about the opportunities for women to get ahead in business, what would they be?

PANELIST: I'm in the most difficult industry for women to break into at the supervisory level, the manufacturing industry, But I think there are many more opportunities now, and they're growing.

Do you think women themselves, more so than men, are preventing women from getting ahead?

PANELIST: Well, that has been our experience. We had a very competent young lady, and the women, I'll have to admit, were the ones who defeated her.

PANELIST: I still feel that women have to be more capable and more efficient to reach the heights that men do.

PANELIST: I think women must still accept the fact that for a certain number of years they must continue to train themselves in order to be superior and in order to get the positions.

PANELIST: And when a woman rises above them [men], they resent it. Don't
             you think this might be one of the things that, if corrected, would
             be going a long way in helping us achieve what we want?

PANELIST: A man just cannot stand it, even though a woman might be as
             humble as all get out and not ever admit that she's done anything.
             Men just naturally resent women going above them.

You think, by the same token, that a man resents having a woman as a supervisor?

PANELIST: I don't find that true. I supervise two men and I don't find that at
             all.

PANELIST: I think it depends on the woman.

PANELIST: I do feel that there are still a good many men who feel that woman's
             place is in the home. Perhaps if she is going to be out in the business
             world, she should not be in a profit-oriented organization
             but rather the educational or social fields, or in the arts, or something
             that will allow her to achieve this self-satisfaction without
             actually competing with men in the profit-oriented world.

PANELIST: I think the women's attitudes as to what they *want* to achieve in
             any field — whether it's in the home or in business — are all important.
             If she's going to be working with men, then she has to
             learn to work with them. I think women can make a contribution
             to business without being in actual competition with men.

PANELIST: You make up your mind where you want to go. If you want to be
             a supervisor, in all probability you're going to be one whether
             there's a man in the way or not. Women are a little bit more devious
             than men in some ways, and they can achieve a goal, I believe,
             if they set out to achieve it.

PANELIST: Our country needs the womanpower that we have, and I don't
             really have any doubts about what women can do. We have more
             jobs available at top levels now and women are needed to fill
             them. The men are filling all they can fill.

PANELIST: We need women who are trained at higher levels. Women just
             can't expect to get jobs with less than a high school education.
             And many times, they must have much more than just high school.

*What do you think women ought to concentrate on more if they're to fill better
jobs?*

PANELIST: Better training and continuing education.

PANELIST: Asking for and expecting better jobs.

PANELIST: And expecting to take the responsibilities that go with the better
             jobs.

PANELIST: I think she's got to "not be a female."

PANELIST: I think you can be feminine and *still* get ahead today.

PANELIST: I'm talking about being "female."
PANELIST: In the derogatory sense.

Do you think that potential women executives feel they've got to be "mannish" in order to be successful?

PANELIST: No, I hope not.
PANELIST: I think this was true in the early 1920s.
PANELIST: I don't think the hard-boiled man gets ahead as fast as he used to.
PANELIST: Maybe you could get the men together now and see what their ideas are that would help us.
PANELIST: I would suggest that you get the two groups together. We would *really* like to know how we can improve ourselves, and how can we know if somebody doesn't tell us?
PANELIST: Well, men still shape business organization and patterns. It's not going to do us any good to be supervisors unless we have somebody to supervise. So no wonder women are interested in finding out what concerns the people under them and what male executives think.

This discussion was a particularly sincere, unemotional, and objective confrontation of problems encountered by women. These women executives were open-minded and willing to recognize and seek constructive advice. They exhibited strong faith in the ultimate potential of women at all levels and in all positions.

They revealed an awareness of the changing dynamics of society's mores and culture. They recognized that rapid changes have taken place concerning the acceptance and status of women in business and as leaders, but that "merit equality" does not uniformly exist at this time.

They focused attention on the handicaps created by the negative attitudes of men, the low expectation women have of themselves, and comparative lower appraisal of women by both men and women.

The discussion revealed that women can and do successfully combine home and business careers; that their lack of acceptance and the attitudes of men are the result of traditional and cultural influences; that women have confidence in their ability to compete and meet the standards required of a job; and that they want to be accepted, evaluated, promoted, and rewarded as individuals, not as women. They are very anxious to measure up to the responsibilities of each position, to the requirements of leadership, and are willing to continue education, exert the effort, and dedicate themselves to their careers to insure their success in all areas.

Index

wives, working, 26
womanpower
  employing and using, 35–73
  inherent promise in, 4
  legal impact of managing, 9–12
  as organized force, 165–167
  see also female employee
women
  absenteeism among, 134–136, 198
  advantages over men, 181
  age and marital status of, 29, 140–141
  age problems of, 136–137
  attitudes of, 104–106
  challenge of roles in, 25–28
  changing roles of, 5
  competition with men, 20
  in computer world, 167–168
  contribution to motivation, 86–95
  counseling of, 124–131
  dedicated career-minded, 140
  dedication to family and home in, 27
  defensiveness of, 23
  development program for, 169–170, 187
  differences among, 22–31
  disadvantages with men, 183
  discrimination against, 10, 171, 185
  dual role of, 5, 25–28, 204
  educational qualifications of, 45
  emotionalism in, 24, 122–123, 126, 137–138, 189
  equal rights for, 166–167
  expectations of, 28–31, 90, 102
  expected role of, 20
  feeling needed, 30
  future role of, 164–165, 192–195
  generalizations about, 66
  great potential of, 67
  handicaps encountered by, 148–149
  high turnover of, 133–134, 197–198
  hourly schedule for, 38
  immediate satisfaction of, 24
  induction of, 51–55
  inexperience of in business scene, 20
  influence of, 14–15
  job-interest stimulation for, 91–92
  job performance of, 31
  job-related problems of, 132–133
  lack of confidence in, 200
  as leaders, 150–151
  leadership potential of, 145–151, 174–175
  leadership qualifications of, 153
  length of employment of, 35–36
  management response to, 12–15
  as managers or supervisors, 149–150, 159, 201–202
  "mannish," 209
  marriage-hopeful, 141

  mature married, 140
  mental deafness in, 79–80
  mood changes in, 63
  "mystery" of, 16–17, 116
  need for purpose in, 30
  opportunities for, 12–14, 170, 207–208
  over 40, 137
  overprotection of, 203
  personal problems of, 45, 139
  practical considerations in opportunity evaluation for, 170
  predictability of, 17–19
  responsibility for own development in, 59
  as richest underutilized resource, 8
  roles and expectations of, 22–25
  search for meaning by, 205
  self-discipline in, 63
  self-identity in, 205–206
  sensitivity of, 23, 61
  short-selling by, 29
  subjectivity and intuition in, 189
  superiority to men, 183–184
  supervision of, 60–67, 172–173, 187–188
  as supervisors, 149–150, 159, 201–202
  taking for granted of, 66
  talkative, 138–139, 188
  training for, 169–170, 187
  unfavorable attitudes in, 109–112
  unique contributions by, 186
  upward mobility of, 152–159, 201–202
  work expectations of, 90
  working with other women, 200–201
  see also female employee
women executives
  barriers to, 186
  interview with, 196–209
  number of, 13–14, 147–148
women in business, assumptions about, 49
  see also female employee
work, motivation through, 90–91
work environment
  attitudes and, 104–105
  favorable, 95
  favorable attitude formation in, 110
  woman's concern for, 62
working, reasons for, 26–27, 44
working wives, number of, 26
working women
  age and marital status of, 29–30
  assumptions about, 180–181
  conclusions about, 171–172
  facts about, 26
  trends and indications regarding, 163–175
  see also female employee; women
World War II
  women as major human resource in, 35
  working women in, 29

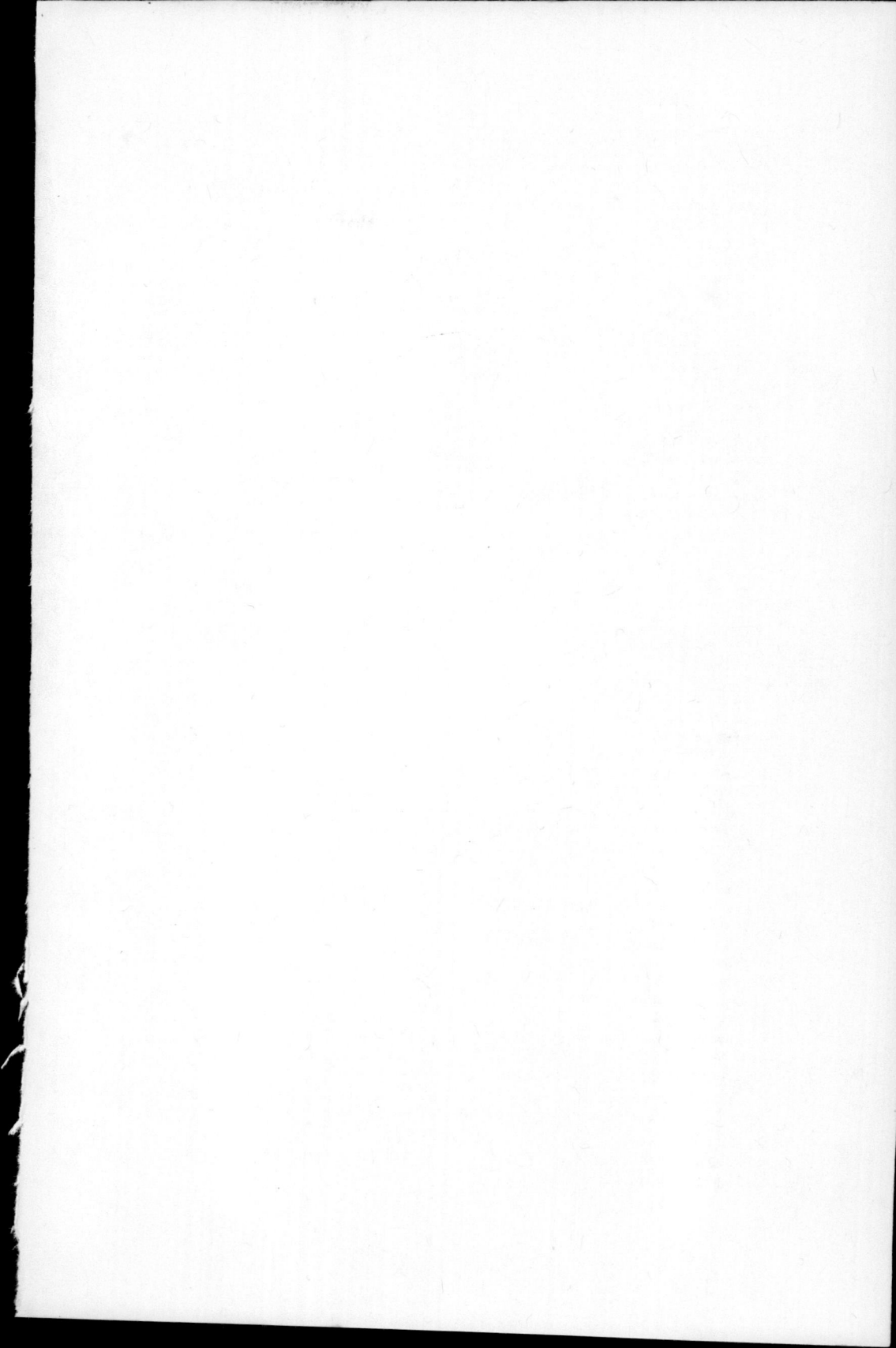

72
74
75
76
79
81
83
85